FALSE
ASSUMPTIONS

FALSE
ASSUMPTIONS

DR. HENRY CLOUD
DR. JOHN TOWNSEND

ZondervanPublishingHouse

Grand Rapids, Michigan

A Division of HarperCollinsPublishers

FALSE ASSUMPTIONS
Copyright © 1994 by Dr. Henry Cloud and Dr. John Townsend

Requests for information should be addressed to:
Zondervan Publishing House
Grand Rapids, Michigan 49530

International edition ISBN 0-310-59577-0

Library of Congress Cataloging-in-Publication Data

Cloud, Henry.
    False assumptions : relief from 12 "Christian" beliefs that can
drive you crazy / Henry Cloud and John Townsend.
        p.   cm.
    Includes bibliographical references.
    ISBN 0-310-59570-3
    1. Spiritual life—Christianity. I. Townsend, John Sims, 1952–.
II. Title.
BV4501.2.C589   1994
248.4—dc20   93-40420
                                                              CIP

Some of the names in this book have been changed to protect the privacy of the individuals described.

Edited by Sandra Vander Zicht and Tim McLaughlin
Cover design by Cheryl Van Andel

Printed in the United States of America

94 95 96 97 98 99 / DH / 10 9 8 7 6 5 4 3 2

To our clients,
who have worked through
all twelve of the
false assumptions with us

Contents

Introduction

This book began with a dilemma.

Time and time again, we'd find that our patients—sincere, Bible-loving believers struggling with emotional issues—had a double burden to bear. Not only were they depressed, or eating compulsively, or having trouble dealing with authority figures, but they were also handicapped by certain teachings that sounded Christian, but weren't.

The ideas appeared true because those who taught them used religious language and quoted Scriptures. These ideas, however, are emotional heresies. They are false assumptions about spiritual and emotional growth. They aren't biblical, and they don't work.

We identified twelve teachings that sound plausible because they each contain a nugget of truth. At some point, however, when Christians try to apply the truths, a breakdown occurs. And the person needlessly suffers.

A woman who suffered from a deep depression because she had been abandoned as a child, was told by a Bible teacher that she simply needed more time with God. She was putting too much trust in people, he told her. Faithfully she tried to follow the principle, "If I have God, I don't need people." She isolated herself more and more from those who loved and cared for her in order to spend time praying and studying the Bible. She spent hours alone, with no human contact.

Eventually, her depression deepened to the point that she was hospitalized. During her stay, after much effort, she learned what the Bible really teaches: that a

9

great deal of God's healing comes through the members of his church.

The most astounding finding of our informal study was that Christians who had been raised with minimal Bible training were less injured by these false assumptions—supposedly biblical teachings—than Christians with extensive Bible training. In other words, Christians who know their Bibles the best are often injured the most. When their allegiance to the Scriptures was combined with dangerous teaching, much pain often resulted.

Though sometimes they questioned their faith, more often they blamed themselves: They weren't faithful to God, or they were secretly resisting what God wanted to tell them. Either way, their emotional symptoms tended to worsen and their pain increased.

The hurting person was then left with one of two options: Leave God and get well in secular psychology, or stay in a Christianity that apparently didn't work and simply cope with being dysfunctional.

As we continued to run across this problem, we searched the Scriptures for answers to these beliefs that were literally driving people crazy. We found that there really is nothing new under the sun: These crazymaking principles have all been addressed in the Bible, from Jesus' confrontation of the Pharisees, who believed that authoritative religiosity was actually the voice of God (Mark 7:5), to John's exposure of the Gnostics, who believed that human connections should be avoided in preference to divine connections (1 John). The Scriptures present clear corrections of all these crazymakers.

Most of these false assumptions have one thing in common: They draw the believer away from God's resources of growth and healing, and toward a system that sounds Christian, but doesn't work.

Several years ago, the Rev. Scott Rae, at that time a

singles pastor at Mariners Church in Newport Beach, California, asked us to speak to his singles group about spiritual growth. We put together a series of Sunday night lessons for an active, questioning group of serious Bible students—and who also wanted honest answers about emotional growth. From that format came the outline of this book.

We wanted to do more than simply react and refute these crazymaking assumptions. We wanted to tell the truth about God's principles of spiritual growth. So in this book we explain the origin of these false principles, show where they go wrong, and present a biblical path for resolving emotional and spiritual problems.

You don't need Bible training to profit from this book. It's written for everyone. But it's meant especially for people who are searching to find out if the Scriptures actually do apply to their sorrows, their conflicts, their emotional growth, and their struggles.

The dilemma can be solved. The Bible can help make you emotionally well, not sicker. God and his Word are part of the solution—not part of the problem.

We pray that you will be able to identify the pseudo-biblical beliefs that can make you crazy. More than that, we hope that you will use the truth of God's Word, of his Spirit, and of his people to grow in grace and in truth.

It's selfish to have my needs met.

Exhausted and lonely one Monday afternoon, Sarah reached over and switched on the radio. It had been a rough weekend. Every request she made of the kids had turned into a battle, and her husband had remained planted in front of the television. She couldn't recall if he had said a caring word to her or the kids all weekend.

It was like the old joke, she thought. "Ask me how my day was," says the comedian.

"All right—how was your day?"

"Don't ask."

It was a bitter joke to Sarah. She didn't even want to think about how depressed she was.

Maybe the radio would help. She flipped through the newspaper for the day's radio listings. The topic on the Christian station was "Help When You're Down." She recognized the speaker's name; he was a local, well-respected pastor. She tuned in the station.

"... so you're down, troubled, lonely, you're under crushing pressure. You wonder sometimes if things will ever change for you."

Is he reading my mind? thought Sarah. He was describing her very feelings at that moment. He understood.

"My friend, there's an answer for you from the Word

of God." Biblically based teaching was important to
Sarah.

"The answer," said the pastor, "is to stop thinking
about yourself and start thinking of others. Just as our
Lord thought not of himself, but emptied himself for
others, we will find joy in self-sacrifice and service. Get
off the pity pot. Repent of your self-absorption, and find
peace in sharing."

Sarah's heart dropped. *Peace in sharing? I've been
sharing myself all weekend, and I'm in pieces, not at
peace.* She had no sooner formed these resentful words
in her mind, than she immediately felt guilty. After all,
the pastor was quoting the Bible. *I guess he's right,* she
told herself bleakly. *I'm just being selfish.*

She reached for the church bulletin to see what
additional committee she could volunteer for. Maybe in
serving more, she'd find the happiness she longed for.
But she was beginning to despair of ever being happy,
of ever feeling satisfied about herself and her life.

Every day sincere, well-intentioned Christians listen to messages similar to the one Sarah heard. That
message—"Stop thinking of your own needs"—is
taught by sincere, well-intentioned Christian teachers
who only want to help people obey the Savior.

The problem is that it's not a biblical message. It
sounds true, but it's not an accurate interpretation of the
Scriptures.

The Root of the Problem

Many of us have been taught a self-annihilation
doctrine for so long that it makes sense to us. After all,
isn't self-centeredness at the core of our sinfulness?
Aren't we supposed to deny ourselves and give sacrificially to God and others?

Certainly, self-centeredness is at the core of our
sinfulness. In Lucifer's heart it all began, as this once-

most magnificent of angels resisted simple obedience, trying instead to put himself above God. Through Adam and Eve, we inherited this tendency to dethrone God and put ourselves in the center of the universe.

This is a serious problem. When we refuse to see God for who he is—and ourselves for who we are—we deny the truth that he is God and we are his creatures. We put ourselves on the throne that only God should occupy. We idolize ourselves. We worship and serve "created things rather than the Creator" (Rom. 1:25).

Not only is it true that self-centeredness is at the core of our sinfulness, but also we are to deny ourselves and sacrificially give to God and others. In fact, Jesus summarized the entire Law and the Prophets under two simple commands: Love the Lord your God, and love your neighbor as yourself (Matt. 22:37–40). Our love for others shows that we belong to God. We are to give from our fullness wholeheartedly as Jesus did. He made himself "nothing, taking the very nature of a servant, being made in human likeness. And being found in appearance as a man, he humbled himself and became obedient to death—even death on a cross!" (Phil. 2:7–8).

So we hear self-denying passages like this in the Bible. We hear the oft-repeated maxim, "God first, others second, self last." And we conclude that the Christian life is a life of ignoring and even hating our own needs, focusing instead on the needs of others.

Yet to believe this is to confuse selfishness with stewardship. This crazy-making assumption—"*It's selfish to have my needs met*"—fails to distinguish between selfishness and a God-given responsibility to meet one's own needs. It's like someone saying, "I saw you last night at the gas station, filling your car's tank. I had no idea you were so self-centered. You need to pray about spending more time filling others' tanks with that gas." Ridiculous, yes—but this is essentially what the

radio pastor told Sarah that Monday morning. Yet if we
don't fill our own tank with gas, we won't get far.

The Bible actually values our needs, which are God-
given and intended to propel us to growth and to God.
Neglecting them leads to spiritual and emotional problems; having them met, however, frees us to meet the
needs of others cheerfully and without resentment.

Let's take a closer look at the biblical view of needs.

Incompleteness

In an old TV commercial for aspirin, a doting mother
helps her grown daughter make dinner. Mom's eager
helpfulness gets annoying, and her daughter's resentment builds. Finally the younger woman blows up.
"Mother, please!" she says, "I'd rather do it myself!"

We're all inclined to do it ourselves. Asking for help
and support is inconvenient and uncomfortable. Sometimes it's unsafe. Yet God built dependency into all of
us. We all need God, and we need each other. "No man
is an island, entire of itself," wrote the seventeenth-
century English poet John Donne. "Every man is a
piece of the continent, a part of the main; if a clod be
washed away by the sea, Europe is the less."

God intended us to be incomplete in and of ourselves. Dependency is built by God into the very fabric
of the universe. Without the sun's warming rays, the
earth would quickly become a frozen tomb. Without
food and shelter from the elements, animals would die.
Deprived of light, soil, and water, plants would shrivel.

Even God reaches out for relationships, though it is
difficult to imagine an all-powerful God with needs. In
his very essence, however, God is a relational being.
He is love (1 John 4:16), and love always has an object.
A lover does not love in the abstract.

So to whom does God reach out for his relational
needs? Certainly not to us. Though God desires close-

ness with us, he doesn't *need* us. This would put the Creator in a creaturely position. He loves and cherishes us, but he doesn't need us.

God exists in a Trinity—three persons in one: Father, Son, and Holy Spirit (Matt. 28:19; 2 Cor. 13:14). His triune nature provides for him constant relationship and connectedness. In a way that we can't imagine, God is always attached, never in isolation. Yet, being God, he is self-sufficient within the Trinity.

Jesus experienced and expressed relational needs. He needed his Father. He "often withdrew to lonely places and prayed" (Luke 5:16; Mark 1:35). He used the expression "Abba, Father" when addressing his Father in heaven, indicating an especially close, intimate relationship to God.

Jesus needed more than his Father—he needed friends, too. Though the primary purpose of Jesus' going to the Garden of Gethsemane was to be alone with the Father, his secondary purpose was to have a select few of his disciples share—at some distance—in his agony. With Peter, James, and John he shared his pain: "My soul is overwhelmed with sorrow to the point of death .... Stay here and keep watch" (Mark 14:34). In his own darkest night of the soul, Jesus reached out to his friends to support him (though they failed to give him companionship).

Incarnational Needs

As God's image bearers, created in his likeness, we also are created to reach outside ourselves to get what we need. But it doesn't stop here. The Bible not only teaches us about our incompleteness, it instructs us about our need for people—"Jesus with skin on."

While many Christians understand that they can't live in a vacuum, they feel uneasy about anyone but God and "spiritual matters" filling that hole up. Yet

God wants us to be loved not only by himself, but by each other. These needs are called "incarnational needs" and will be dealt with more fully in chapter 7.

Why incarnational? Because Jesus stands alone in all the religions of the world. He became man—flesh (incarnation), to make an attachment to us *just as we are.* He showed us that God wants to connect with people, as a person. As John says, "That which was from the beginning, which we have heard, which we have seen with our eyes, which we have looked at and our hands have touched—this we proclaim concerning the Word of life" (1 John 1:1).

Christianity is unique in that, while other religions involve humankind reaching up to God—in Jesus, God reaches down to our level. In other words, Almighty God reached down and baptized human connection by sending Jesus. Just as he hungered, thirsted, and felt loneliness, so can we.

Our incarnational needs are taught all through the Bible. For example, after he created Adam, God saw that it wasn't good for him to be alone (Gen. 2:18), so he created Eve. God built human beings to need him and to need each other. "Pity the man who falls," says the Preacher, "and has no one to help him up!" (Eccl. 4:10) One of the most spiritual activities you can perform is to need other people.

Our Needs Are Logical

In the daily hospital psychotherapy group that I was conducting, some of the group members were depressed, some had anxiety disorders, some had compulsive and addictive problems. All were Christians, and all spoke about learning to depend on others for their emotional neediness.

The conversation upset Raymond, however, who had been in the hospital for three days. He suffered from severe depression. He resisted coming into the program because he felt like a spiritual failure. In his mind, a depressed Christian was a backslidden Christian.

"This subject of needs just isn't valid," Raymond protested. "We are to minister grace to the world and get our minds off that nonsense."

"So it's important to minister to the world?" I asked.

"Absolutely. We are to give comfort, encouragement, and hope to those with don't have it, in the name of Jesus."

"I certainly have no problem with that," I said. "But do *you* also get comfort, encouragement, and hope?"

"That's selfish," he replied. "God doesn't want me concentrating on myself."

"Then God's using you to hurt people."

"*What?*"

"If your need for comfort, encouragement, and hope is selfish, then others' need for that is selfish, too. If it ain't okay for you to *have* it, it ain't okay for you to *give* it."

Gradually Raymond's theology changed—and so did his relationships with his wife and kids. He learned to accept his own neediness and to reach out and ask for help when he needed it.

The assumption "It's selfish to have my needs met" makes people crazy not only because it hurts people, but because it isn't true. It isn't logical, and it doesn't make sense. To give a cup of cold water to those who need it, we need to have drunk from it ourselves. If we are to forgive, we need to have been forgiven. Paul says it best:

> Praise be to the God and Father of our Lord Jesus Christ, the Father of compassion and the God of all comfort, who comforts us in all our troubles, so that we can comfort those in any trouble with the comfort we ourselves have received from God. (2 Cor. 1:3–4)

Our Needs Are Designed to Drive Us to Growth

Scientists have tried for years to invent a perpetual motion machine, one that can operate indefinitely without fuel or maintenance—but with no success. It would be nice if we could all be perpetual motion machines, with no need to ask for help, no need to call a friend when we're depressed or panicked, no need to ask advice when our finances go awry, no need to talk to someone when our eating is out of control or our marriage is shaky.

Our neediness forces us to realize that we are creatures, that we must look up at God in humility and ask him for what we need. Our humble position is designed to drive us closer to God, to others, and ultimately to maturity, "attaining to the whole measure of the fullness of Christ" (Eph. 4:13).

Jesus' story of the Pharisee and the tax collector makes this point:

> Two men went up to the temple to pray, one a Pharisee and the other a tax collector. The Pharisee, standing by himself, was praying thus, "God, I thank you that I am not like other people: thieves, rogues, adulterers, or even like this tax collector. I fast twice a week; I give a tenth of all my income." But the tax collector, standing far off, would not even look up to heaven, but was beating his breast and saying, "God, be merciful to me, a sinner!" I tell you, this man went down to his home justified rather than the other; for all who exalt themselves will be humbled, but all who humble themselves will be exalted. (Luke 18:10–14 NRSV)

The Pharisee was "standing by himself," boasting of his good works. But the tax collector would not even look up to heaven. He recognized his sins and inadequacies, and they drove him to God.

If you don't recognize your needs, you stagnate. You

have little reason to seek God. Those with no symptoms don't seek a doctor. It's easier to deny your mortality when you don't suffer from high blood pressure, weight problems, or shortness of breath. Start putting on weight, though, or experience dizzy spells, or have to gasp for breath—*then* you call the doctor. Similarly, when you feel lonely and depressed, *then* you draw closer to others and to God. There will always be more demand for curative than preventive medicine.

Our needs place us, then, in the position of having to ask for help. Just as thirst leads us to drink and hunger forces us to find food, our spiritual and emotional neediness compels us to reach for someone else. The tax collector asked for mercy, and he "went down to his home justified" (Luke 18:14).

Our Needs Are Designed to Drive Us to Humility

As long as we think we're better than most, we will rarely admit our needs and ask for help. We distance ourselves from other people, like Edom. The Edomites sought security in being distant and uninvolved, but their pride proved deceptive (Obad. 1:3). As the Bible points out, "A man's pride brings him low" (Prov. 29:23).

Jim and Brenda came to me for marital help. It was soon clear to me that Jim was emotionally self-sufficient to a fault. When Brenda took the kids on an out-of-state trip to see her mom, Jim would call every day to see how they were doing, but he'd never admit that he was lonely and that he missed them.

When Brenda asked how he was doing, Jim would say, "You know me—I'm fine. Couldn't be better. You guys have a great time."

Brenda knew her husband, but only after a fashion. She knew that nothing threw Jim. She knew that he weathered job losses, physical ailments, and friendship conflicts with nary a frown. She knew that he didn't need help from anyone.

Finally, Brenda had had enough. She dragged him to couples therapy. "I don't know why Jim married me," she complained. "I don't feel like I matter to him. Sometimes I wish he'd have some huge tragedy just so he'd ask me for help."

Jim seemed arrogant to his wife because he'd been trained that way. Jim's father had been absent when he was young, and his mother was dependent and immature. He learned early not to depend on anyone else. For him to cry and be lonely or sad was too much for his weak mother, who'd spiral into depression. So Jim suppressed his negative feelings as well as the experience (but not the need) of needing others. He also became resourceful and responsible.

Ironically, his resourcefulness and sense of responsibility was tough on his marriage. Brenda had no neurotic "need to be needed." She simply wanted to know her man. But his resistance to being vulnerable made him appear to be arrogant and self-satisfied, further isolating her from him.

It wasn't until Jim began seeing his self-sufficiency as pride instead of responsibility that he began changing his behavior and rebuilding his marriage.

We are responsible for ourselves. We all carry our own load of cares, obligations, and problems. The apostle Paul tells us: "Each one should carry his own load" (Gal. 6:5). This is *functional independence*, in which state you carry out your normal responsibilities. You don't ask others to work for your living, or to pay your bills for you.

At the same time, however, we are *relationally dependent*. We all need to be loved. It's the fuel of life. Being connected to God and others keeps us going. We need empathy, comfort, understanding, and reassurance from others. Jim had learned to be both functionally independent (this was healthy) and relationally independent (this was unhealthy). He needed to cultivate a relational dependence; he needed to need others. That is humility. "A man's pride brings him low, but a man of lowly spirit gains honor" (Prov. 29:23).

Humble people know they can't do it all themselves, for humility teaches them to ask for help. They know they must reach out to survive. That's why the Bible tells us that God "mocks proud mockers but gives grace to the humble" (Prov. 3:34).

Our Needs Are Designed to Draw Us Closer to God

Answering an attack from the Pharisees, Jesus said, "It is not the healthy who need a doctor, but the sick. But go and learn what this means: 'I desire mercy, not sacrifice.' For I have not come to call the righteous, but sinners" (Matt. 9:12–13).

God doesn't rescue perfect people. He wants people with problems. People with nothing to fix have nothing to say to God. Those who are poor in spirit, those who are in mourning, those who are meek—those are blessed (Matt. 5:3–5) because they can be filled, can be comforted, can be helped. He never said, "Blessed are those who have their act together." If nothing is broken, nothing can be fixed.

We are drawn to this gospel message because we have problems. And after joining a church, we spend our next forty years trying to hide our problems. Having no problems is a problem.

The self-righteous attitude of thinking we have no problems is what birthed Alcoholics Anonymous in the 1940s. People found that in A.A. meetings they could still have struggles; they could still be needy. In fact, they had to confess their shortcomings at *every* meeting. The church today is making great strides in embracing this biblical attitude. The church should be a place where it's safe to be unfinished, incomplete, and needy.

Neglecting Our Needs Leads to Spiritual and Emotional Problems

If God built us with needs, then it stands to reason that letting our needs go unmet can cause major problems. Just as neglecting regular oil changes will destroy your car's engine, neglecting our God-given, legitimate needs will cripple us.

Karen, a professionally dressed woman in her thirties, came to see me about her depression. Concentrating on her work and sleeping were equally difficult, she told me. She had withdrawn from family and friends; suicidal thoughts occurred to her more and more frequently. A complete physical had revealed nothing wrong. In severe depression, Karen felt despairing and hopeless. And she hadn't a clue about its cause.

During our first session, I explored Karen's past and present relationships. Karen had maintained a high position of leadership in her local church, was active in her community, and was a wonderful wife and mother. Yet nearly every significant person in Karen's life—her mother and father, her sister, her best friend from high school, her college boyfriend—had either abandoned her or had no emotional attachment to her.

She'd married Peter, a good man who nevertheless was unable to make deep emotional connections (just like Karen). His workaholism kept him away from home a lot; but in some ways, that was a relief to both of them. "Because we rarely see each other," she said, "we appreciate each other more when we're together."

Their kids were being raised by caring parents who didn't know how to receive what they were giving. And the children were having problems. Their nine-year-old daughter tended to be socially withdrawn, and their teenage son was beginning to run with the wrong crowd.

The more Karen talked, the clearer the picture became. Her personal emotional isolation was repeating itself in her marriage and her church. For decades she had been running on emotional empty, getting along only on her strong will, guilt, and adrenalin. Now she needed to learn the humble task of filling her spiritual tank up—with God and with people.

After I gave Karen my diagnosis, she asked, "Isn't there a book I could read, or a seminar I could attend?"

"As disconnected as you are now," I said, "your depression will get worse, no matter how many books you read or seminars you attend."

Karen took the scary, risky step of learning how to connect, how to ask for help, support, comfort, and understanding. It wasn't easy, but she worked hard for a long time. As she became more humble, as she recognized her needs and began to ask for help to get them met, her depression gradually lifted.

Karen's depression signaled to her that she needed something outside of herself—at least a book or a seminar, she thought. She responded to the signal and learned how to be needy and poor in spirit. God provided the symptom and the resources; Karen worked at learning to ask.

Psychological symptoms are God's way of letting us know that something is wrong. Depression, anxiety, eating disorders, substance abuse, and compulsive behaviors are all symptoms of a deeper problem. These symptoms the Bible calls "fruit": "Likewise every good tree bears good fruit, but a bad tree bears bad fruit. A good tree cannot bear bad fruit, and a bad tree cannot bear good fruit" (Matt. 7:17–18). In other words, bad fruit is not the problem, but only a symptom of the problem. We need to dig until we find the root of the problem, then heal that. We must pay attention to our psychological, spiritual, and relational symptoms, for they let us know if we are getting our needs met.

Getting Our Needs Met Helps Us Meet the Needs of Others

The false assumption that it is selfish to have our needs met is very seductive to Christians, probably because all of us want to be loving, caring people. Yet our desire to give ourselves to others is what some teachers use to scare us into thinking that taking care of our needs will drown us in a whirlpool of self-contemplation, hedonism, or narcissism.

Nothing, the Bible says, is further from the truth. Having our needs met frees us to meet the needs of others—without resentment. Having a full stomach spiritually and emotionally allows us to give cheerfully (2 Cor. 9:6–7).

The most comforting people in the world are those who have been comforted; the most understanding people are those who have been understood; and the most loving people, those who have been loved. The disciple whom Jesus loved the most (John 21:20) unsurprisingly became known as the apostle of love. What he received, he later gave.

Jesus confronted Simon the Pharisee with this truth when a prostitute, overcome with God's grace, washed Jesus' feet with her tears: "Therefore, I tell you, her many sins have been forgiven—for she loved much. But he who has been forgiven little loves little" (Luke 7:47). Having found forgiveness, the woman was able to love much, whereas Simon the Pharisee was blind to his own neediness and was therefore unable genuinely to love.

Contrary to what the radio preacher had so vigorously taught, Sarah began meeting her own needs first.

She resigned from a few committees. People who depended on her did without her while she got help. Most important, when she was in need, instead of calling and offering to help, she called and asked for it.

"It's really different," she told me. "I didn't expect what has happened to my ministry. Hour for hour, I probably do less for others than I used to, but what I do is light years better. For the first time in my Christian life, I actually *want* to help. I *want* to serve. I don't feel resentment or guilt. I think I'm actually learning what being loving feels like."

One could do worse than sit at the prostitute's feet and learn from her. The Pharisees in your life may want you to stay away from reminders of your neediness. You do need to adhere to their *truly scriptural* teachings (Matt. 23:2–3), but as you grow more and more aware of your deep and desperate incompleteness, of your need for love from God and from others, you truly become— as the prostitute did, and as Sarah is doing—more like the Master.

Ask yourself, "Am I asking for what I need?" You may need support in a crisis, or advice about a problem, or comfort in a loss. All these needs the Father of the heavenly lights welcomes. "Every good and perfect gift is from above" (James 1:17), and they often reach us through other people (Acts 9:6–19).

If I'm spiritual enough, I will have no pain or sinfulness.

Ted was discouraged. He was becoming more and more depressed every day, so much so that he had begun wondering if he were really a Christian. So he increased his Bible study and prayer and listened to all the spiritual-life tapes he could get his hands on.

His depression only got worse. And he began wondering if his life was even worth living. With nowhere else to turn, Ted sought professional counseling.

"I just don't get it," he admitted to me. "I've studied the Bible and diligently tried to obey it. I exercise as much faith as possible. I memorize Scripture. I try to make right choices. I've sat under the best Bible teachers in the world. But I'm still so depressed I can't function."

"What do you mean, you don't get it?" I asked him. "Why should all those things keep you from depression?"

"If a Christian is really walking with the Lord, he won't get depressed like this," Ted reasoned. "Depression is always the result of some spiritual failure. Only I can't figure out what I'm doing wrong."

What Does Pain Have to Do with Goodness?

Ted is not alone in his thinking. Many Christians believe that if they have their spiritual lives together, they will not suffer from emotional problems and will somehow avoid sin. If pain or sin invade their lives, they conclude that something is spiritually wrong with them.

The false assumption under which these Christians suffer is this: *"If only I am spiritual enough, I will have no pain or sinfulness."*

When these people do hurt, they cannot explain it. Have they failed? Has God abandoned them? Should they do something different spiritually to make the pain go away? Are they being punished for some sin?

People under the cloud of this assumption see only two options: try harder at the spiritual disciplines, or give up on the spiritual life altogether.

The Example of Job

Perhaps the best-known individual who learned this lesson was the biblical character Job. His losses were horrific: possessions stolen or destroyed, servants murdered, children crushed to death under a collapsed house, his body covered with excruciating sores.

Like Ted, Job wondered why. How could a loving God allow these things to happen? He had done everything right, and yet he suffered unimaginable pain.

As his depression deepened, Job wished only to die: "I prefer strangling and death, rather than this body of mine" (Job 7:15). This hero of the faith was not living what we would call an abundant life.

When Job's infamous friends came to comfort him, they were quick to voice this false assumption.

> Should not your piety be your confidence and your blameless ways your hope? Consider now: Who, being innocent, has ever perished? Where were the upright ever destroyed? (Job 4:6–7)

In other words, you will be protected from pain if you are truly holy.

> Does God pervert justice? Does the Almighty pervert what is right? When your children sinned against him, he gave them over to the penalty of their sin. But if you will look to God and plead with the Almighty, if you are pure and upright, even now he will rouse himself on your behalf and restore you to your rightful place. (Job 8:3–6)

In other words, you suffer because you sin. If you are truly good, you won't hurt.

> Yet if you devote your heart to him and stretch out your hands to him, if you put away the sin that is in your hand and allow no evil to dwell in your tent, then you will lift up your face without shame; you will stand firm and without fear. You will surely forget your trouble, recalling it only as waters gone by. (Job 11:13–16)

In other words, if you depend wholly on God and stay away from sin, your pain will go away.

> Yield now and be at peace with Him; thereby good will come to you. Please receive instruction from His mouth, and establish His words in your heart" (Job 22:21–22 NASB)

In other words, the remedy for your pain is to yield to God and study his Word.

The message Job received from his friends is familiar: You suffer because you have failed spiritually. Get your act together, and then God will bless you and deliver you from your pain.

Because their message to Job was neither biblical nor real, God rebuked his friends: "I am angry with you ... because you have not spoken of me what is right, as my servant Job has" (Job 42:7).

Yet every day Christians are just as sure that they're

suffering because of something they did wrong. And their friends can be no more helpful than Job's: "You'll feel better when you become more spiritual."

To the contrary, God tells us that we will encounter sin and pain within ourselves, others, and the world around us every day—even if we have regular daily devotions and we go to church twice on Sunday. Being a Christian does not exclude you from problems and pain.

But I Shouldn't Have These Thoughts

Susan's husband was in his final year at seminary, preparing for the pastorate. Despite a zeal for calling, the seminary years had been difficult. Susan and Sam had three children under four years of age, very little time to themselves, and never enough money.

Susan struggled to be what she called "a good Christian wife and mother." She never complained about how difficult things were. After all, hadn't she been taught that she could do all things with God's help?

But this was her problem: She had an obsessive fear that she would throw her children out of the car while driving. At first she ignored these thoughts, hoping they would go away. But mental pictures of this act persisted, so she tried memorizing Bible verses about prayer and a pure thought life.

Never abating, the thoughts continued to disturb her so much that she no longer dared drive the children anywhere. She became housebound. Terrified, she came in for counseling.

We talked about where the thoughts might be coming from. "Have you ever considered that you might be angry about all of your responsibilities with the children," I asked Susan, "and that at times you would just like to be rid of them?"

The question jolted her. "Be rid of my children? Never! I love them very much. How could you even suggest such a thing?"

"I didn't suggest that you do not love your children. I just suggested that you might be angry at how difficult things have been for you and Sam, and that at times you might resent how much you have to do."

"It's not right to be resentful," she said. "That's not a fruit of the Spirit. You shouldn't feel that way, so I don't."

"I understand that resentment is not a good feeling, and that it is not a fruit of the Spirit," I replied. "But I think at some level you must resent your children, or you wouldn't be thinking about throwing them out of the car window."

"But I can't feel that way," she said. "It's not right."

"Do you think that you only feel 'right' things?"

"Well, that's what you're supposed to do," she replied, less sure of herself. "You're supposed to feel love, patience, joy, and things like that. Not resentment and hatred for what you have to do."

"But what do you do when you do feel hatred and resentment?"

"I don't let myself feel things like that. You shouldn't. It's not godly."

"What if it were okay to feel those feelings? Do you think that those feelings might be there then?"

"But it's *not* okay. That would be sin."

"What makes you think you are without sin?" I asked.

She looked trapped.

Susan's responsibilities, lack of support from her husband and friends, and her unmet needs overwhelmed her. No wonder she was angry. And denying her anger only produced irrational thoughts. As she slowly understood what the Bible truly says about our negative sides, she found not only the freedom to admit that she was full of resentment, but also the courage to find solutions to her problems.

Susan found some safe people to whom to express all the pain, hurt, and anger she had buried for so many years. All of her activity, she discovered, had been only a strategy to keep herself from feeling pain. Yet as she brought her pain to the surface and let it be touched by loving people, she found she didn't need all the busyness in her life.

Susan's picture of a loving person—one who said yes to anyone with a need—began changing, too. It was not sinful to say no to other people's requests, Susan began to realize. A lifetime of shoulds—she should be patient, should serve others before herself, should not be angry—had kept her from solving deep problems. Now, with permission to not always put herself on the back burner, to reserve time for herself, to be angry, she could face the truth and begin solving the real problem: her anger at her powerless situation. Regaining power and self-control in her life eliminated the anger. In addition, when she did have sinful feelings and attitudes, she felt free to admit them.

These changes inside Susan soon became visible. So she learned to set limits on her husband's unrealistic demands. She began to ask friends and family for help when she needed it. She didn't wait until she got sick before feeling she could take time for herself. Instead of trying to be wife, mother, teacher, neighborhood minister, and church administrator, Susan adjusted her expectations of herself so they were more reasonable.

In short, Susan recognized her anger and hurt, letting them stimulate her to solve problems in her relationships, rather than letting them fester and turn into bitterness.

Ways We Try to Avoid Pain

Caught in a trap, Susan felt two contradictory truths: "I should not feel this way. I do feel this way." What do you do when you uncover feelings in yourself that "good Christians" aren't supposed to feel? Or when you find yourself doing things a "good Christian" should not do?

There are three common ways we handle our negative feelings and behaviors if we don't allow ourselves to own them.

Denial

When Susan denied the feelings she believed she shouldn't feel, her denial produced obsessive thoughts.

King David recognized this truth when he prayed to God: "Search me, O God, and know my heart; test me and know my anxious thoughts. See if there is any offensive way in me, and lead me in the way everlasting" (Ps. 139:23–24). He suspected he had offensive ways in him. So instead of denying them, he wanted to face the truth. He did not fear his badness, for he knew that the grace of God was big enough to handle it.

Besides producing psychological symptoms such as depression or anxiety, denial compels us to judge others because we cannot see them clearly. We often criticize others harshly for things we deny in ourselves: "You, therefore, have no excuse, you who pass judgment on someone else, for at whatever point you judge the other, you are condemning yourself, because you who pass judgment do the same things" (Rom. 2:1).

The Bible clearly teaches we are wrong to deny our sinfulness. Again and again Jesus points out our need to confess and face our sinfulness. "What comes out of a man is what makes him 'unclean,'" Jesus taught. "For from within, out of men's hearts, come evil thoughts, sexual immorality, theft, murder, adultery, greed, malice, deceit, lewdness, envy, slander, arrogance and folly. All these evils come from inside and make a man 'unclean'" (Mark 7:20–23). Jesus wants us to own our real feelings, not cover them up with religious activity.

Those that *did* deny their sinfulness, Jesus confronted: "Woe to you, teachers of the law and Pharisees, you hypocrites! You clean the outside of the cup and dish, but inside they are full of greed and self-indulgence. Blind Pharisee! First clean the inside of the cup and dish, and then the outside also will be clean" (Matt. 23:25–26).

Denial is clearly not a biblical option: "If we claim to be without sin, we deceive ourselves and the truth is not in us" (1 John 1:8). The good news, however, is that we are safe in the love and grace of God. We can own our badness and not fear condemnation.

Works

Another way we try to handle our bad sides is by working harder, usually to make up for our faults, improve ourselves, or ease our guilt. The Bible calls this "salvation by works" (Eph. 2:9); we try to save ourselves by working harder. More accurately, we try to perfect and sanctify ourselves by working harder (Gal. 3:3).

Joe tried this. He truly hated Scott. Yet whenever Joe felt his own hostility rising, he would instantly feel guilty and ashamed.

Instead of admitting his hatred and trying to resolve it, he put his hostility out of his mind and tried instead to be especially kind toward Scott. In his courteous behavior, Joe told himself, he had "put on the new self" (Eph. 4:24). His forced civility toward Scott, Joe reasoned, was truly righteous and holy. The problem with this approach to his dark side, though, was that he never owned and confessed his old self first. He tried to work himself out of his hatred instead of confessing it.

The more he tried to be nice to Scott, the more Joe found himself slandering Scott behind his back or saying sarcastic things about him. Trying harder was not making him a more loving person.

One day Joe came across this verse in Proverbs, and immediately knew what he had to do: "He who conceals his hatred has lying lips" (Prov. 10:18). He saw that his flattery and kindness was merely a cover for his hatred.

We try other works as well—reading the Bible and praying daily, for example, thinking that these alone will somehow transform our inner selves. But religious efforts like these done by rote, without facing our problems, are useless. They become empty rules, lacking "any value in restraining sensual indulgence" (Col. 2:23).

The Law

Another trick we pull trying to deal with our badness is to "put it under the law"—that is, condemning it, feeling guilty about it, and getting angry at it. We actually believe our guilt will cause us to change.

Becky tried putting her envy of her sister "under the law." She was too healthy to deny her feelings and impulses, but whenever she felt envious, she got angry at herself and said, "I'm so bad." She would get angry at herself for failing to control her negative feeling, and then try to scold herself into feeling more loving. (See False Assumption #9 for a more complete treatment of how guilt fails to change us.)

Guilt is a key feature of the law. As Paul and others frequently mention in their letters, the law brings wrath, makes us sin more, holds us prisoner, and condemns us as complete failures when we break even one point of the law (Rom. 4:15; 5:20; 7:5; Gal. 3:23; James 2:10). The law has an angry nature to it; and when we are angry with ourselves and condemn ourselves for our sinfulness, we are acting out the law of sin and death. We are destined to repeat this pattern until God overcomes it with grace (Rom. 7:9–10).

But guilt and condemnation are helpful, some Christians maintain, leading us to confession. The Bible is very clear, however, about the destructiveness of guilt. Christ died to set us free from condemnation; it has no place in the life of the believer (Rom. 8:1).

These methods of dealing with our sin—denial, works, and the law—are all fruits of the false assumption that if we are Christians, we will have no sinfulness.

Not All Negative Feelings Are Sin

Denying our sinfulness is natural. Who wants to claim ugly sins such as bitterness, envy, or hatred?

But what about negative feelings that are *not* sinful—the ones that result merely from living in a less-than-perfect world or from getting sinned against? What is one to do with pain, grief, anger, sadness, or fear that results from sexual, physical, or emotional abuse as a child?

Some in the church say that to still suffer from these things indicates unrepented sin. The sufferer is accordingly condemned for feeling pain.

This was the message that Job heard from his friends. But contrary to it, he was just a victim of circumstances. Tragic events befell him. Though some of his ideas about God may have been distorted, his sin did not cause his hurt. Enormous loss did.

When we feel hurt and anger over what happens to us, we need to respond to our pain correctly. The Bible talks about the importance of dealing appropriately with sadness (see Rom. 12:15; Eccl. 3:4; 7:2–4). It talks about how to deal with anger (see Eph. 4:26–27). It explains how suffering refines us (Rom. 5:3–4; Heb. 2:10–11). But nowhere does the Bible say that pain resulting from an act against you is sin. Nowhere.

Yet in some Christian circles, victims of child abuse, divorce, and emotional abuse are told that, because they feel pain from past hurts, they are somehow not appropriating the sufficiency of the gospel—and are therefore sinning. (Such teaching is actually close to Christian Science doctrines, which deny the reality of pain and sickness.)

To blame victims for their pain is a sin against the wounded, against the brokenhearted, against the oppressed; it is a sin against God himself, whose heart is with those who hurt (Ps. 34:18). Throughout the Bible God sides with the wounded victim. Scripture commands us to heal the brokenhearted: "And we urge you, brethren, admonish the unruly, *encourage the fainthearted, help the weak,* be patient with all men" (1 Thess. 5:14 NASB, emphasis mine).

Nowhere does Scripture tell us to confront the wounded. It tells us instead to love them. Admonition, we are told, should be reserved for those who are unruly or rebellious (1 Thess. 5:14). Job, the model sufferer, gave us clear advice about approaching those who hurt: "For the despairing man there should be kindness from his friend; lest he forsake the fear of the Almighty" (Job 6:14 NASB).

Too often the church confronts hurting people about their pain instead of treating them with kindness and compassion. Because of this false message, the wounded person forsakes God and the church.

The Fallout of This Teaching

If you are taught that spirituality means no pain or sinfulness, you will bear bad fruit—in particular, fruit such as feelings of failure, wasted energy, hiding, unforgiveness, and lack of love.

Feelings of Failure

The Bible makes failure normal for us. "We know that the law is spiritual," says the apostle Paul, "but I am unspiritual, sold as a slave to sin. I do not understand what I do. For what I want to do I do not do, but what I hate I do. . . . For I have the desire to do what is good, but I cannot carry it out. . . . So I find this law at work: when I want to do good, evil is right there with me" (Rom. 7:14–15, 18, 21). It is normal to fail. To teach that people should be without pain or sinfulness puts them under great and undeserved guilt for failing—for being normal, struggling, human sinners.

If the only way I can deal with my pain is to deny it, by trying harder to not feel it, or by condemning myself for it, I am setting myself up for failure. The Bible, however, offers us the freedom to accept our problems and the freedom to face them.

Wasted Energy

Because trying harder to overcome pain and sin is another way of dealing with this false assumption, it is inevitable that such Christians waste their energy. Their white-knuckle efforts only demonstrate that they are compensating for personal sinfulness they have not yet accepted. Remember Jesus' words: "For whoever wants to save his life will lose it, but whoever loses his life for me will save it" (Luke 9:24). Human effort never transformed anyone.

Hiding

The only viable answer to sinfulness is repentance, forgiveness, and grace. We must bring our badness and pain "into relationship with God and others" to be healed (1 John 1:9; James 5:16). We bring our badness into relationship by repenting and asking for forgiveness. Only then do we receive grace. If we believe that it is unacceptable to stumble and fall, then we will do what Adam and Eve did when they fell out of relationship with God—hide.

When we are severed from the love of God and others, we hide. Unless we believe that it is okay to reveal badness and pain to the grace of God and his church, it will never be healed. What we hide is not in light, but in darkness (Eph. 5:13–14), and it cannot be transformed by the grace of God. Healing always comes through unconditional acceptance, which comes only through relationship.

Unforgiveness

If people hide the pain of their past, they cannot forgive those who injured them. Yet forgiveness is God's way of taking the power out of past hurts.

Wounded and hurting Christians who are taught to forget their pain and sins against them have not yet gone through the forgiveness process. They bury unforgiveness in their heart. Yet to get on with forgiveness and untie ourselves from those who hurt us, we must name and feel the sins against us. If you forbid dealing with pain in your past, then you forbid forgiveness.

There are other traps, too. Some teachers give only lip service to forgiveness by advising you to forgive *as an act of the will*—despite the fact that the Bible tells us to forgive with our *heart* (Matt. 18:35). It takes more than an intellectual forgiveness of those who betrayed us. We must forgive them with our whole being—mind and emotions, as well as will.

This is, after all, how God forgave us. He expressed

his anger, sadness, and hurt. He named the sin against him, and he let it go. He is our model.

This false assumption—denying pain and badness—blocks people's ability to follow Christ's model. Some have forgiven with their will, but in their hearts still lurk pain and anger.

Furthermore, when we are out of touch with our own sinful nature, we will not experience the forgiveness of God. Many people understand the fact of their forgiveness, but they do not feel it emotionally. They are hiding their real selves, including their sinful nature, from God and others.

We can know in our hearts only what we have experienced. If we have not experienced the love and forgiveness from God and others, then grace will not have its full effect on us (1 John 1:9; James 5:16). If you sidestep your own sinfulness, hiding it from God and others, then you probably won't avail yourself of the grace of God. Nor will you be able to extend forgiveness to others. The Bible says we forgive others based on having first received forgiveness from God (Matt. 18:23–35; 1 John 4:19).

Lack of Love

We are not born with the ability to love; we learn by being loved, by seeing love modeled. "We love because he first loved us" (1 John 4:19). Furthermore, Jesus teaches that our ability to love is tied to how much we have been forgiven. To the generous love of the prostitute who washed his feet, Jesus pointed as evidence of being forgiven much. Then he warned, "But he who has been forgiven little loves little" (Luke 7:47).

If we believe that spirituality is the absence of sinfulness, we are out of touch with our sinfulness. If we are out of touch with our sinfulness, we are out of touch with our need to be forgiven (like Simon the Pharisee). If we have been forgiven only of little, then we love only little.

The more we face our shortcomings and bring them to grace, the more loving we will become. People who are comfortable confessing their own sinfulness because God and his people are gracious become more and more loving people. Love is a fruit of forgiveness.

You Will *Suffer Pain, You* Will *Sin*

If it is erroneous to believe that Christians should have no pain or sin, then what *does* the Bible teach?

The exact opposite—that we *will* have pain, that we *will* sin, and that, because of the grace of God, we are free to face these things.

If confession is agreeing with the truth, then we must understand the Bible's truth about badness.

1. *Sinfulness is normal.* Expect failure. That is why Jesus had to die for us, after all. To believe we can become perfect after we become Christians is denying our fallenness (1 John 1:8). So expect to find within you all that Jesus mentions in Mark 7:20–23. But do not fear it. Own it, because God is gracious.

Seeing sin as normal does not contradict other teaching about becoming victorious over sin. It means only that as long as we're on earth, we can expect to be sinners.

2. *Negative feelings are normal, not sinful, when they arise from a sin against you.* It is natural to feel angry when someone betrays you, or hurt when someone lies to you, or sad when someone omits your name from the party list. We will inevitably have pain to work through, for example, if we have been sexually or physically abused, or if we suffered the loss of a parent. To get well, we must process these normal responses to being hurt in a fallen world (Eccl. 7:3–4).

3. *We need to deal appropriately with both sets of feelings.* We must confess and forsake our *sin*—our envy, jealousy, bitterness, pride, and being judgmental. We must also take our *pain*—our sadness, grief, hurt, abandonment, woundedness, and rejection—to God and to others, where it can be loved and healed.

This is what David speaks of in the Psalms of healing (see Ps. 13; 30; 31:9–19; 32; 38; 102; 103:1–5). He poured out his heart to God and gave thanks for his deliverance (Ps. 116:5–9). Likewise, after we receive grace, we must forgive those who have wronged us. Freedom from the past is both receiving and giving grace.

4. *The gospel is grace, and we must grow in it.* Any feeling or behavior that we feel condemned for is a signal that we have not accepted the grace of God.

In short, we need to accept the presence of badness in us. We need not fear it, for Christ died for us. He made it safe for us to own our badness and not fear it anymore. Through that gospel, he brings us back together with him and others. As the writer of Hebrews tells us:

> Let us draw near to God with a sincere heart in full assurance of faith, having our hearts sprinkled to cleanse us from a guilty conscience and having our bodies washed with pure water. Let us hold unswervingly to the hope we profess, for he who promised is faithful. And let us consider how we may spur one another on toward love and good deeds. Let us not give up meeting together, as some are in the habit of doing, but let us encourage one another—and all the more as you see the Day approaching. (Heb. 10:22–26)

Because God accepts our fallenness, we can too. We need not hide anymore. We can take our fallenness to each other and to God, and through those safe relationships find healing that leads to love and good deeds.

If I change my behavior, I will grow spiritually and emotionally.

A knot in her stomach, Debra piloted her minivan into the driveway. She knew what awaited her inside: sullen, resentful children and a critical husband. Barry and the kids weren't bad people—but no one in the family was getting along these days.

Yet much of the blame rested on her shoulders, Debra thought. She hadn't been much of a wife and mother lately. Tired and depressed, she had to force herself out of bed in the morning to get ready for work and to fix breakfast for Barry and the kids. In her most dejected moments, she had even thought, "What's the use of going on?"

Reaching out for help, Debra poured out her story to Sharon, the wife of an elder at their church and known for her piety. "The worst part," Debra concluded, "is that I just don't feel like being the positive one in the family anymore. I can't pull it off."

The older woman nodded her head sympathetically. "Debra, your negative feelings are coming from a lack of caring acts. Emotions always follow behavior."

"But what can I do?" Debra asked.

"Reverse the process. If you act loving, you'll feel loving. So act more loving toward Barry. Do special things for the kids. Do one helpful act for each person every day. Smile more. You'll be amazed at the changes in your heart. The Bible says we're to 'put on the new

45

self"—and that means to behave like a loving Christian.
Then you'll *feel* like a loving Christian."

It seemed dishonest to Debra to act differently than
she felt, but she was desperate. So that night she
walked into the family room of their home, saw Barry
sitting in his easy chair, took a deep breath, and told
herself to apply Sharon's words. "Hi, honey!" she said
cheerfully. "I'm making pepper steak for you and the
kids tonight."

Barry and the kids enjoyed both the dinner and
Debra's bright attitude. There was only one problem:
Debra still felt depressed. She felt better for a few
minutes after behaving lovingly, but that's all.

"It's like I'm falling down a deep tunnel into
blackness," she told me a few days later. "Every now
and then I'll do something positive, but it feels like I'm
only digging my fingernails into the wall of the tunnel.
My nails can only hold on so long."

The Behavior Trap

Many Christians seeking help are plagued by this
third supposedly biblical idea that can make you crazy:
"If I change my behavior, I will grow spiritually." This
crazymaker says that behavior change is the key to
spiritual and emotional growth. As Debra's older friend
put it, "The more we act right, the more we feel right."

This teaching holds that our emotions will simply
fall in line as we behave better and better. For example,
to feel loving towards someone, act loving. To combat
depression, act happy and think positive thoughts. To
deal with angry feelings, behave kindly toward others.
To overcome destructive habits (compulsive eating,
substance abuse, money problems, sexual addictions),
just say no to that piece of cake, the glass of wine, a new
pair of jeans, that pornographic magazine.

This false assumption, taught widely among Christians, has been deeply influenced by the behavioral school of psychology, which believes that all that counts is actions. Over time, behaviorists say, behavior can change feelings.

So What's the Problem?

Of course, there's a grain of truth in this scriptural-sounding crazymaker. Aren't we're supposed to "spur one another on toward love and good deeds" (Heb. 10:24)? How can doing good deeds be a problem?

The problem is not doing good deeds, but the role doing those deeds plays in our spiritual and emotional growth.

Problem #1: Changing only our behavior confuses fruits with roots.

Over and over again, the Scriptures point out that our actions are the *result* of spiritual change, not the *cause* of it. Good behavior is the cart, not the horse. Changes in behavior, such as becoming more loving or more responsible, indicate that God is doing an invisible, internal work of grace within us, transforming us to be more like him "with ever-increasing glory" (2 Cor. 3:18).

Look at all the ways that God wants to bear fruit in us: "The fruit of the Spirit is love" (Gal. 5:22); "the fruit of the light consists in all goodness, righteousness and truth" (Eph. 5:9); "And this is my prayer: that your love may abound more and more in knowledge and depth of insight, so that you may be ... filled with the fruit of righteousness that comes through Jesus Christ" (Phil. 1:9–11). Paul asks God to fill the Colossians with the knowledge of God's will so that they "may live a life worthy of the Lord and may please him in every way: bearing fruit in every good work, growing in the knowledge of God" (Col. 1:10). Positive behavior, whether it be defeating a compulsive eating disorder or working in a soup kitchen, comes from God's work in our hearts.

In fact, the Bible sees destructive behaviors not as the cause of a bad attitude, but as the *result* of the heart's sinful condition. "For the sinful nature desires what is contrary to the Spirit. . . . The acts of the sinful nature are obvious: sexual immorality, impurity and debauchery; idolatry and witchcraft; hatred, discord, jealousy, fits of rage, selfish ambition, dissensions, factions and envy; drunkenness, orgies, and the like" (Gal. 5:17, 19–21). In other words, problems inside us result in selfish, hurtful acts.

If doing good deeds—that is, changing my behavior—does not lead to spiritual and emotional growth, what does?

The answer lies in this fact: Spiritual and emotional growth doesn't occur all at once. Just as we physically pass from infancy to toddlerhood to youth to adolescence and, finally, into adulthood, we also pass through specific developmental stages of our emotions: bonding to others, separating from others, sorting out good and bad, and becoming an adult.[1]

Bonding to others. Bonding to others, or attachment, is our deepest and most primary spiritual and emotional need. God is relational, and he created us as relational beings (1 John 4:16). From the womb, we need connection with God and others for comfort, safety, a sense of belonging, nurturing, and meaning. People who are injured during this developmental stage, who do not bond as infants and children, have great difficulty trusting, being intimate, and depending on others. As a result, they may become depressed or may compulsively overeat, trying to find comfort in food rather than in the love of others.

Separating from others. Our second developmental need is to separate from others in order to take ownership of our lives. We must learn what is us and what is them. We must learn to distinguish between what God has and has not given us responsibility for. This principle of learning responsibility applies all the way from taking care of the earth (Gen. 1:28) to saying no when a friend asks you to lend him money that you have pressing, legitimate need for yourself. In this developmental stage we need to learn the skill of setting limits, or boundaries, around our personal spiritual property.[2]

People who are injured during this developmental stage—those who have inadequate personal boundaries—often can say no only with great difficulty. They have trouble staying focused, getting organized, and controlling their lives. They may fly into a fit of rage, suffer a panic attack, or get depressed when they feel overwhelmed by all the projects and people for which they feel responsible.

Sorting out good and bad. After learning how to say yes to love (bonding), and no to evil (establishing boundaries), our third developmental need is to resolve the problem of good and bad. It is in this stage that we learn that we and the world aren't black and white. We learn that we are imperfect people living with imperfect people in an imperfect world. From holding impossible ideals for ourselves and others, we move to grieving over our losses, forgiving others, and receiving forgiveness ourselves. Jesus said that he didn't come for the well, but for the sick (Matt. 9:12). When we accept our sinfulness as something that draws us to Jesus, we are becoming wise. Those who are injured in this third stage often struggle with perfectionism, overoptimism, denial, and shame. They feel that life isn't fair. The fruits of this kind of injury can include bulimia or sexual addiction, in which the "bad" part of a person's character becomes sexualized, causing him or her to act out sexually.

Becoming an adult. In this final stage, a person moves from emotional childhood to emotional adulthood. God desires that we be mature and take authority over what he has given to us: our gifts, values, careers, marriages, friendships, and callings. No longer can we depend on the approval of parents; as emotional adults, we value their input, but make our own way in the world. As Jesus said, we have only one Father, and we should not call anyone on earth "father" (Matt. 23:9). People injured during this fourth developmental stage, who do not grow up, either have problems submitting to authority, or they are overcompliant and rule-bound. They either question authority at every turn, or they never do. They either break the rules, or they follow them to the letter. The fruit of such injuries includes scrapes with the law as well as obsessive-compulsive disorders, in which a person has a persistent preoccupation with an unreasonable idea (like worrying about getting fired or getting cancer) or has an irresistible impulse to perform an irrational act (like frequent hand washing).

Many people are damaged during all four stages. For example, you might have trouble making attachments with people. So you set to work on that—only to discover in the process that you can't set limits with others. And this inability, in turn, causes you to avoid people instead of confronting them. Your isolation consequently increases.

You might also become keenly aware of what psychologists call a *good-bad split* in you, which causes you to condemn yourself any time you experience failure or loss. This only makes you withdraw further from others. At the same time, you may cave in to those in authority around you, afraid to challenge them or voice your opinion. Your fear of criticism from your superiors may further distance you.

In all these cases, destructive actions do not cause, but *follow* spiritual and emotional problems. Yes, we are responsible for what we do; but we must recognize the source of our actions before we can change them. Let's "clean the inside of the cup and dish," as Jesus said, "and then the outside also will be clean" (Matt. 23:26).

The process of belatedly leading yourself into emotional adulthood can be discouraging at first. But as you deal with all the issues, you are deepening and strengthening your bonds with your support network. You are working work step-by-step and shoulder-to-shoulder with a patient God, who wants you to handle only what you can handle today (Matt. 6:34). The result? A gradual increase of your loving feelings, of your emotional connections, and of your loving attitudes and behaviors toward others. And then your fruit will begin changing.

Behavior is a spiritual barometer. It reflects change more than it causes change. The Bible teaches that what we do and how we behave reflects who we are. "A good tree cannot bear bad fruit, and a bad tree cannot bear good fruit ... by their fruit you will recognize them" (Matt. 7:18, 20). In other words, we are to observe the results of our lives—our actions—and evaluate if they are good. Then we'll have a handle on evaluating our spiritual state.

For example, the giver who allows others to control her time often appears fruitful. People speak well of her loving actions. Yet her fruit is actually a halfhearted, resentful compliance (2 Cor. 9:7). If she continues to give reluctantly, depression or compulsive behaviors will surely follow. Depleted, she will begin to emotionally and spiritually withdraw.

Depression and compulsive behaviors are often blessings in disguise. These distressing symptoms signal that something is wrong inside, and that we need to seek help. What a contrast to the idea that we are to "behave" well to get well! The Bible teaches us just the opposite: Getting well brings better behavior.

How then do we grow spiritually and emotionally? Just as the correct mixture of sunlight, water, air, and soil nourishes a plant through its seed, shoot, bud, and adult states, we also need ingredients to help us grow. God provides three elements that nurture our passage through the four different stages of growth: grace, truth, and time.

Grace. Grace, the first ingredient necessary for growth, is something we get from God. We don't deserve grace; we can't earn it. God just gives it to us. God created us to need relationship, and when relationship was broken in the Garden of Eden, he restored us into relationship with him through grace. "When we were God's enemies," the Bible says, God "reconciled [us] to him through the death of his Son" (Rom. 5:10).

Despite the violent problems spawned by gangs in urban centers throughout the country, it is in gangs that many young people, ironically, find grace. Here they are accepted. They may have been kicked out of their childhood homes, they may have run away from home, they may feel alienated. To compensate they chose a new family, albeit a destructive and damaging one. But they feel permanently attached. As a thirteen-year-old girl said about the prospect of being killed in a gunfight, "At least I'll die with my gang."

Grace says you belong, no matter who you are or what you do. You are part of the family. You matter. A safe relationship can fuel your spiritual and emotional growth. Just as the branch can't survive long without the vine (John 15:6), you can't flourish without being spiritually and emotionally attached and connected to God and his people.

Truth. If grace is the heart of growth, truth is its skeleton, its structure. Truth is the information we must learn to live life. Truth may nudge us to assume responsibility in one area or to confront the sin in another. Truth may impel us to learn a new skill, like setting boundaries. The truths of the Bible, for example, relate to our need to be "thoroughly equipped for every good work" (2 Tim. 3:17).

Phyllis came to therapy disturbed that she preferred her nine-year-old daughter over her twelve-year-old son. The active boy constantly rubbed her the wrong way, frequently challenging her authority. Phyllis discovered that she resented him daily. The girl, on the other hand, was helpful, cooperative—just more likeable.

It wasn't that Phyllis didn't understand her son's boyishness. She understood his need for more controls. She also recognized that he and her daughter were at different developmental stages. Yet try as she might, Phyllis couldn't *make* herself feel closer to her boy.

One day in therapy, Phyllis realized that her son reminded her of a lost part of her personality. She'd been raised to be compliant—very much, in fact, like her own daughter. Her parents had discouraged any disagreement in the house. Phyllis's son revived in her deep feelings of self-hatred, which in turn reflected her hatred of her parents for rejecting her innately aggressive and challenging nature.

The truth behind her feelings liberated Phyllis. Now that she knew where the feelings originated and why her son pushed so many angry buttons in her, she could deal with her feelings and learn to love her son more. In addition, she began to develop the sassy part of her personality she had buried in childhood. The truth had indeed freed her (John 8:32).

Time. Time is the incubator in which grace and truth produce their fruit. Time allows us space to learn the maturing truths we need, with no condemnation. When Jesus told us to take up our cross daily (Luke 9:23), he was referring to, among other things, the ongoing process of taking ownership of our lives. Spiritual growth is not instantaneous. It's more like what an oven does than a microwave, slowly and gradually heating and melting the ingredients together to produce a new person.

Phyllis, for example, didn't change her feelings for her son overnight. It took time to deepen her understanding of her own fear of being aggressive, time to distinguish her son's behavior from her past, time to get to know him in a new way, time to forgive her parents. But slowly and gradually, she began to accept her son with more grace and less resentment.

These three elements unite in our lives to make us recovered, whole, loving, and functional beings. Grace and truth come to us through Jesus (John 1:17), and one purpose he makes of them is to mature us.

Like Debra, Jeff was depressed. The thirty-five-year-old businessman couldn't concentrate on work, had no energy, and couldn't sleep at night. Fights with his wife were getting more frequent.

"I feel like I'm a walking dead man," he said during his first therapy session. "I can't feel alive. I can't feel sadness. I can't feel my wife or my kids. And I want to."

The Christian therapist diagnosed an attachment disorder; in other words, Jeff had difficulty making emotional connections. So at some point in life, he learned to cope by being competent, responsible, and self-sufficient.

In weekly sessions with his therapist, Jeff found a

safe place to explore why feelings and closeness were so difficult for him. He also joined a relationally oriented Bible study at his church, where he gradually opened up and began sharing his deepest fears and desires.

Through a difficult process, Jeff came to terms with the fact that he came from an emotionally detached family. Though he had always thought his parents were near perfect, he began to see that their perfection was merely polite distance. Then he felt in himself loss and anger.

Jeff also had to learn to take responsibility for his disconnection. Although he did not cause it, it was *his* problem, not the problem of his parents, his wife, or his friends. He had to take ownership for every time he withdrew when he should have reached out for comfort and help. With his support group's help, he became acutely aware of all the ways he maintained distance from others.

All three elements of growth gradually fell into place for Jeff: grace (through his therapist and support group), truth (in the form of the biblical information he learned and how it applied to the insights of those who knew him), and time (as week after week he dealt with his tendency to withdraw rather than reach out to family and friends).

Growth is a process. We need a safe place of love, helpful information about ourselves, and time to practice and fail.

What does this view of growth tell us? Simply that good, mature, loving, responsible behavior follows God's pattern—it comes after long, hard periods of work on root issues.

Consider this scenario: You contract a fever and visit your doctor. He diagnoses you with a bacterial infection. Then, instead of writing up a prescription for an antibiotic, he looks you in the eye and says, "Here's

how to cure your fever: Three times a day, act 98.6
degrees. Behave as though you had a normal temp. I'll
see you in a couple of weeks."

Remedies as unsound as this are urged on Christians
when they're told to change their fruit—while ignoring
the root.

*Problem #2: Changing only our behavior forces us
first into phariseeism, then into despair.*

In essence, the elder's wife told Debra to pretend
she loved others. So Debra tried to cover up her
conflicts. This covering up of resentment—the spiritual
thing to do, according to Debra's friend—sounds omi-
nously like what the Pharisee did, and what Jesus
reserved some of his most harsh words for.

> Woe to you, teachers of the law and Pharisees, you
> hypocrites! You clean the outside of the cup and dish,
> but inside they are full of greed and self-indulgence.
> Blind Pharisee! First clean the inside of the cup and
> dish, and then the outside also will be clean (Matt.
> 23:25–26).

The Pharisees had it together. They behaved correctly in all circumstances, on all occasions. They were
scrupulous. Yet judging from Jesus' words to them, God
is more interested in Debra's understanding why she is
depressed (so that she can resolve her depression) than
he is in meticulous correctness. He is more interested
in our searching our hearts (Ps. 139:23) to find out why
we act out, are sad, or have impure thoughts. He wants
to get at the actual problem—the spiritual problem—
and heal it, because he knows that then and only then
will the outside of the cup be clean.

Some people can pretend good behavior for a while.
Like actors waiting in the wings to perform, they ready
themselves for acting happy and positive, for behaving

correctly, for appearing spiritual. It takes lots of effort, too.

People who extend their pretend existences for a lifetime often control others by becoming their teachers, just as Sharon, the elder's wife, controlled Debra. Such control keeps the Sharons of the world away from their own problems. Debra, however, was headed in another direction. Despite Sharon's "behavior" answer, Debra was headed for despair.

When our hope is not realized, we despair: "Hope deferred makes the heart sick" (Prov. 13:12). That's what happens to some when they attempt to live life according to this crazymaker. Years and years of trying to do the right thing, of trying to behave in right ways— yet with no deep sense of emotional connectedness to God or others—sooner or later loses steam. These disappointed and frustrated people often leave the church—Christianity "just didn't work out," they say. They feel like spiritual failures because they couldn't act "like a Christian."

Yet the very word "Christian" signifies "problems." We are saved only when we are aware of our grave spiritual trouble, only when we are convinced we can't live life on our own without God. Christians, then, behave like everyone else—that is, like people with problems. We may be forgiven, but we're not perfect.

The distinction Jesus pointed out between the prayers of a Pharisee and a tax collector illustrate this. The Pharisee fasted, tithed, and thanked God that his behavior was proper. The tax collector simply pled for mercy with a humble and repentant heart—and left justified (Luke 18:10–14). Beware of those who seem to have their spiritual act together. They may recruit you to their fasting and tithing program, without checking first with God.

Problem #3: Changing only our behavior denies the power of the Cross.

The "good behavior" approach insults the redemptive power of God to heal us. It places the power for change squarely back onto our shoulders. It assumes that we have the power to stop our selfish, lustful, hating hearts—by changing our behavior. (See Assumption #10.)

Changing one's behavior in order to change one's heart also fosters a proud, omnipotent self-dependency that leaves God out of the picture. Instead of God, all we have is an impotent deity who feebly wishes us well while passively watching our pain and struggle.

This is hardly the case. God is the source and being for our recovery: "For from him and through him . . . are all things" (Rom. 11:36). He is at work within us "to will and to act according to his good purpose" (Phil. 2:13). He forms, fuels, and forges our growth and emotional repair.

This teaching that "If only I change my behavior, I will grow spiritually and emotionally," is, at its heart, an idolizing of humans. Colossians 2:23 calls this "will-worship" (NKJV), or the worship of our willpower, our own power to sanctify ourselves. It turns its face from humility, from dependency on God and on his church. It turns its face from inability, from brokenness, and from failure. And it depends on our own internal power to choose maturity every time—a power we lost at the fall.

How Should We Then Behave?

If changing your behavior does not produce long-lasting differences in your spirit, then should you simply "let go and let God"? Should you become a passive observer in your own spiritual recovery? Should you sit back and let God fix you?

This perspective isn't any more biblical than the "behavior" answer, its opposite. God places a high value on personal responsibility—the part we have to play in our growth. We are to "work out [our] salvation with fear and trembling" (Phil. 2:12).

Remember that God wants to help you develop an increasing sense of responsibility over your life. He wants you to become fully adult. Children need others to be responsible for them; but to grow into emotional and spiritual adulthood is to become stewards of our feelings, thoughts, and behavior.

Then what can we do? If both are true—that our actions are signals that indicate our spiritual condition (rather than causes that determine our condition), and also that we bear responsibility in getting well—then what can we do to help ourselves without trying to do God's work for him?

The Bible presents an answer: Instead of attempting to fix our symptoms, we can actively take ourselves to good nutrients. Just as a tree planted in rich soil can flourish, so can we expose ourselves to God's healing resources.

The only behavior we can practice that will move us to emotional and spiritual adulthood is picking ourselves up and taking ourselves to good nutrients—that is, to God and his people. Yet even this action on our part is God's work within us: "No one can come to me unless the Father who sent me draws him," Jesus said (John 6:44). It's hard to admit that we are powerless to change our behavior. It takes deep humility to take our failure, shame, and pain to the right kind of people— people who will move toward us, comforting us as they themselves were comforted (2 Cor. 1:3–4).

The alcoholic who tries to stop drinking by using willpower and commitment is wasting his time. He's much better off using that willpower to take himself to the next support meeting. The depressed individual who tries to act positively is stuck in a cycle of despair. She needs to find places of grace and truth where her weary heart can find healing. As we use our behavior to propel us to love and responsibility instead of trying to fix ourselves, we use our actions to bring about true change.

Actions Can Be Confusing

Yet even positive behavioral change can actually be a warning that all is not well. And negative actions can actually be a *good* sign of growth. Even no change can be a sign of growth.

The "Sprinter": Resentment-driven Bursts of Good Behavior

Frank sat on the edge of his seat during his first session of therapy, painting himself a picture of eagerness and cooperativeness. You wouldn't have thought that a man whose wife had kicked him out of the house until he got therapy would be this positive about getting help. You wouldn't have thought that a man with a long history of rage attacks, work performance problems, and chronic lateness would be this eager for help. Yet he seemed to be just that.

"Just tell me the program, Doc," Frank told me. "I'll do whatever you say."

"Okay," I said. "It's pretty simple. The program is this, Frank: Disagree with and rebel against everything I say."

There was a long pause. "Why?" he finally asked.

"Because it will help you stop lying," I told him. "Your lifelong history shows that you can't disagree with others until you feel pushed against the wall. You have tremendous needs to be approved, and yet you hate complying in order to get approval. I'm suggesting we see who you really are."

Frank also had a long history with therapists. First persuading them that he was a highly motivated client, he would then improve his behavior significantly, attributing it to the brilliance of the therapist. Then for no apparent reason, he would "relapse"—lose his job, get in a fight, or terminate therapy abruptly.

Frank's sudden burst of positive behavior had nothing to do with his spiritual development. He was merely appeasing a feared and hated authority figure. Years earlier, I discovered, Frank had learned to placate his angry father the same way. Frank was a man pleaser instead of a God pleaser (Gal. 1:10). And it never stuck, because it was based on the fear of disappointing someone rather than on gratitude for being loved. Frank had learned to sacrifice his true feelings to avoid the anger of others.

Frank didn't say much the rest of that first session, but during the second one he had plenty to say. He began telling the truth about how deeply he resented having to see me, how angry he was at what he perceived as his wife's leveraged power play, and ultimately how afraid he was of being controlled by others.

Initial bursts of good behavior are often based on fear. However, no growth comes unless love is present—and love and fear can't live in the same heart: "There is no fear in love. But perfect love drives out fear, because fear has to do with punishment" (1 John 4:18). For Frank, doing the right thing was only a way to keep from being hurt. There was no fruit of love in his heart.

When Worse Means Better

The second reason we can't always trust behavioral change is that what looks like regression is sometimes a good sign. For example, Frank finally underwent a period during which he was more oppositional, rebellious, and hard to live with than ever. Some Christians would have assumed he was only backsliding and needed to be confronted with his sin.

Yet Frank was in the process making the outside of the cup consistent with the inside (Matt. 23:25–27), bringing out conflicts and injuries he'd been hiding for years. And as he began responding to attachment and to nonpunitive limits, he was able to bring his behavior under control.

Spiritual and emotional injuries and deficits are often hidden in darkness inside our hearts, away from relationships marked by the grace of God and his people. When these painful and negative thoughts and memories begin emerging in relationships, people sometimes act for the first time as they have actually felt for decades.

Some get angry. Some mourn their losses. Some feel dependent for the first time in their lives. Such feelings can be unpleasant for both the person feeling them and for those around him or her. But expression of these feelings indicates that God is bringing what has been in isolation into relationship.

The story of the prodigal son and his "good" elder brother points this out. After the younger son had squandered his inheritance in wild living, he felt empty and realized his need for help. However, the elder son—the "good" one—was full of envy: "All these years I've been slaving for you and never disobeyed your orders," he lashed out at his father. "Yet you never gave me even a young goat" (Luke 15:29).

In other words, the elder son behaved well because

he feared losing the inheritance, not because he wanted to be good. The prodigal son, however, dealt honestly with his sinfulness and rebellion and was able to repent and be close to his father.

What appear to be dangerous and even bad periods in some lives can actually bring them closer to the Lord, because these individuals honestly wrestle with God, as did Jacob at Jabbok, rather than fearfully comply.

No Change Isn't Necessarily Stagnation

When one gets emotional help, there may be no immediate results. Depression hangs on. Their eating is still out of control. The marriage still teeters on the edge.

At this point, well-meaning friends often enter the scene to say something like this: "If your therapy [or support group, recovery program, etc.] is working so well, why aren't you different? Isn't it supposed to produce results?" The person in recovery begins to doubt the process, his own intentions, or God himself.

Again, spiritual and emotional growth isn't instantaneous. In Scripture God continually compares our maturity and recovery to how plants thrive: the one who delights in God's law "is like a tree planted by streams of water, which yields its fruit in season" (Ps. 1:3).

What is your "in season"? "In season" means "at the proper time." Given the proper ingredients for growth, such as hard work and God's inner working, you will burst forth with fruits of the Spirit: love, joy, peace, and self-control (Gal. 5:22–23). "In season" means not a day before—and not a day later. Premature fruit is willpower driven, not God driven.

You'll go through dark times, times when your behavior still feels out of control, times when you might question God. But he is still working deep within your character, moving, healing, and changing you inside. Like the farmer scattering seed and seeing it sprout "though he does not know how" (Mark 4:26–29), you don't always know how God is changing you. But keep doing your part, and let him have his way with his ingredients, deep inside. Easy change is shallow change, not character growth.

A season of no change in your life may simply mean that some particularly important and deep healing is going on inside right now. Beware of those who might interpret God's slow, underground, invisible work in you as a sign of no growth. Beware of promises of quick fixes that require nothing of humility, faith, patience, or delay of gratification—all signs of true spiritual maturity.

Debra, the budding behaviorist whose predicament opened this chapter, was fortunately a searcher. When her resentment and anger weren't alleviated by her "good" actions (as her friend assured her they would be), she didn't keep trying the same thing.

But neither did she give up. She got involved in a recovery group at church that gave her permission to understand her negative feelings instead of discounting them. She found a Christian therapist who helped her see that acting positively was simply that—an act. And she found the grace to resolve the feelings.

Pepper steak even found its way again to Debra's dinner table—not to assuage her pain, but because she loved her husband and kids.

I just need to give it to the Lord.

Alcoholism had cost Dennis two large businesses and two families. After each loss my friend built himself a new life, but he was unable to sustain it. A wife would divorce him, a business would go bankrupt.

Binges, police interventions, and drunken stupors had often embarrassed Dennis and his families. Many mornings he woke up in places he could not recall having driven to. His life was bleak, and his friends had little reason to believe he could ever change.

Dennis is a different man today. No longer the alcoholic of twenty years ago, he is a successful businessman, a good husband, a loving father, and a faithful friend. He leads a ministry to addicts in his church and is known in the community for responding quickly in seemingly hopeless situations.

The fruit of his current life is remarkable. Nor is this a short-lived, religious turnaround: he has maintained his current lifestyle for two decades.

Curious about how he had made the turnaround in those early, hopeless days, I asked him once how he became sober.

"It wasn't hard," he said dryly. "I went to seven AA meetings a day."

Clearly, Dennis's recovery had not just dropped out of the sky. He had worked very hard at it, discovering that God requires us as his partners in sanctification, in the process of making us holy. This is especially true in significant emotional growth, which God says is a partnership between him and us. Not choosing to do it alone, he has devised a system whereby he works *with us* to mature us, heal us, and develop us into the image of his Son (Rom. 8:29; 2 Cor. 3:18). He requires us to be active, responsible participants in our own healing.

Listen to how Paul says it: "Therefore, my dear friends, as you have always obeyed—not only in my presence, but now much more in my absence—continue to work out your salvation with fear and trembling, for it is God who works in you to will and to act according to his good purpose" (Phil. 2:12–13). Indeed, "we are God's workmanship, created in Christ Jesus to do good works" (Eph. 2:10).

In other words, we are co-laborers with God in working out our salvation. Though his part is primary, we have an indispensable, distinct part also. We are stewards of our own salvation and sanctification.

Many Christians, however, adopt a passive attitude toward their spiritual and emotional growth, especially if they struggle with emotional pain, character weaknesses, life situations that need changing, or dreams that need to be realized. Such Christians often have a "let go and let God" view of their healing and growth process.

This belief—"*I just need to give it to the Lord*"— can make and keep Christians crazy.

To the contrary, there is an active role for us to play in spiritual and emotional growth. Many Christians are stuck because they do not perceive themselves as partners with God in cultivating their own growth.

Not Opposites, But Parallel Truths

It is a paradox that many believers understandably have trouble comprehending: We are unable to save ourselves, and we must be active participants in our process of growth and change.

On one hand, the Bible says that if we try to save our lives, we will lose them (Matt. 16:25). We are unable to change by ourselves, and we are by nature "dead in [our] transgressions and sins" (Eph. 2:1). In a profound sense, it is God who both initiates our salvation and carries it to completion (Phil. 1:6; Rom. 11:36).

With only this truth (that we cannot save ourselves) and without its partner (we must be active participants in our salvation), sincere believers will ask God to heal their depression, take away their anxiety, deliver them from bulimia. Haven't they turned to him as Savior, to one who gives them abundant life? They are disappointed, confused, and frustrated when God fails to deliver the abundant life they requested.

The parallel truth to our powerlessness is that we must aggressively press forward, diligently working out our salvation in order to lay hold of that which God has secured for us. The Bible is clear in explaining the active role we must take in our own growth:

> Be diligent in these matters; give yourself wholly to them, so that everyone may see your progress. (1 Tim. 4:15)

> Fight the good fight of the faith. Take hold of the eternal life to which you were called. (1 Tim. 6:12)

> I press on toward the goal to win the prize for which God has called me heavenward in Christ Jesus. (Phil. 3:14)

If I do not do my part, growth will not happen.

A Pair of Passive Teachings

There are two popular teachings on emotional recovery.

"Position" Teaching

"You just need to focus on your position in Christ. He has secured everything for you. He is sufficient. If you truly believe your position in Christ, you will escape the undesirable emotional state you're in."

The first idea, which I call "position" teaching, emphasizes that if we really knew what God has secured for us in the heavenly realms, we would be transformed into a state of wholeness. We should not have to deal with hurts from the past, or any other pain or brokenheartedness.

This misrepresents the process of sanctification. God *has* secured an eternal position for us in heaven and *has* blessed us with every spiritual blessing (Eph. 1:3), but Scripture also teaches that *we must go and possess what he has secured.*

This is analogous to what we are told in the Old Testament. There we read that God secured the Promised Land, but the Israelites still had to fight deadly battles to possess what he had secured for them.

Listen to the way God described it to Moses:

> Speak to the Israelites and say to them: 'When you cross the Jordan into Canaan, drive out all the inhabitants of the land before you. Destroy all their carved images and cast idols, and demolish all their high places. Take possession of the land and settle in it, for I have given you the land to possess. . . . But if you do not drive out the inhabitants of the land, those you allow to remain will become barbs in your eyes and thorns in your sides. They will give you trouble in the land where you live." (Num. 33:51–53, 55)

The idea is this: God has secured a position of health and Christlikeness for us, but we must fight the fight with him to possess that position. If we do not, then the old inhabitants of our soul will continue to plague us. We must be actively involved in our sanctification. Teaching Christians that all they must do is "know their position and security in Christ" denies their responsibility for the process—the responsibility to face their pain and the issues that caused it.

This teaching keeps many from doing the things the Bible says to do. It sounds spiritual, but in reality these believers are avoiding responsibility. We have seen many people who have suffered for years with emotional disorders, trying to get relief through "realizing their sufficiency in Christ," without doing the hard work required for real transformation. When they do begin to do the hard work, other Christians attack them for being secular humanists and living apart from faith. Many have been hurt by this deception.

Trying desperately to realize their "security in Christ," they fail to achieve real security, which comes from deepening our relationships with God and his church and from growing in character and abilities. They need to be "rooted and established in love" (Eph. 3:17), and "speaking the truth in love, [they] will in all things grow up into him who is the Head, that is, Christ. From him the whole body, joined and held together by every supporting ligament, grows and builds itself up in love, as each part does its work" (Eph. 4:15–16).

"Get Your Eyes Off Yourself" Teaching

"You just need to get your eyes off yourself and on the Lord. All the introspection you're doing is self-centered, humanistic, and just plain useless. Introspection is self-worship. Just focus on the Lord."

Not only are Christians admonished to internalize their position in Christ, but they are told to get their eyes off themselves and onto Jesus. "Stop being introspective," their friends tell them. "Stop thinking of yourself," their pastor warns them. This teaching sounds so spiritual that it's hard to disagree with—

largely because the Bible *does* warn against self-worship.

But prohibiting individuals from looking inside themselves distorts Scripture. The Bible, in fact, says the opposite. The Bible teaches that we must look inside and work on the things in our soul. In fact, Jesus says that looking at ourselves is the first thing we should do: "You hypocrite, first take the plank out of your own eye, and then you will see clearly to remove the speck from your brother's eye" (Matt. 7:5).

David was introspective in Psalm 139 when he asked God to help him look inside and find out what was wrong (vv. 23–24). Early in the Psalms he confessed that God desires truth in the "innermost being" (Ps. 51:6 NASB). Paul is a further example when he says, "A man ought to examine himself before he eats of the bread and drinks of the cup. . . . But if we judged ourselves, we would not come under judgment" (1 Cor. 11:28, 31). These teachings do not call for humanistic self-worship, but a godly examination of ourselves.

Scripture records that whenever people encounter God, they end up looking inside themselves, at all that is wrong within them. His grace gives them the permission, and his holiness forces the comparison. When Isaiah saw God, he immediately saw also the desperate condition of his own heart (Isa. 6:1–5). James clearly describes the process of humbling ourselves before God: "Come near to God and he will come near to you. Wash your hands, you sinners, and purify your hearts, you double-minded. Grieve, mourn and wail. Change your laughter to mourning and your joy to gloom. Humble yourselves before the Lord, and he will lift you up" (4:8–10).

As we gaze at God, we get in touch with our sinfulness and brokenness. Those who teach us to get our minds off ourselves are actually teaching us to avoid the process of cleansing, healing, and sanctification.

The Bible teaches that spiritual growth is an extremely self-involved process; we must continually be looking at ourselves through confession, cleansing, and repentance. Contrary to what an anti-counseling movement is saying, this kind of introspection is no secular-humanistic self-glorification. We are not to glorify ourselves, but to humble ourselves before God so that he can transform our soul into his likeness.

Gaining self-awareness includes confessing our sins and gaining truth in our innermost parts. When we find the aspects of the self that need to die, we put them to death. But this is impossible without self-awareness and looking inside.

Twelve Steps and Other Confusion

"For years I fought my depression and eating problems by trying to change," Jane told me, "but I got worse instead of better. Then I went to a twelve-step group at our church, and they said that I had to admit that I was powerless to change, and that I could not do anything on my own. God would have to change me. Now I come here and you tell me that we have a lot of work to do! I don't understand."

"Both are true," I said. "You are powerless, and you have a lot of work to do."

"But if I'm powerless to change, what in the world am I supposed to work on? It doesn't make sense."

As the Twelve-Step movement has grown in the church, Christians like Jane are confused about what we have the power to do in our own sanctification. If we are powerless, as Step One teaches, what can we do to make ourselves holy? If we are poor in spirit, as the Beatitudes tell us, what can we do to recover from emotional and spiritual pain? Admitting we are powerless begins to sound a lot like "letting go and letting God," doesn't it?

In a sense, yes. Without God's help, we are powerless to heal our pain and transform our ingrained
patterns. The processes of healing and transformation
are mystical; we cannot control them. "Night and day,"
Mark writes, "whether he sleeps or gets up, the seed
sprouts and grows, though he does not know how"
(4:27). We cannot *will* healing or growth; like a growing
plant, with the right ingredients, it happens.

In another sense, however, we can be a good
gardener. We can guard our hearts, making sure that we
submit ourselves to the process, that we get the
nutrients God has provided, that we endure the weeding and pruning he suggests, that we absorb the water
and sunlight of his love and grace and truth.

In fact, there are at least a dozen tasks that we have
the ability to do in cultivating our own growth.

1. *We have the ability to own our problems.* This is
called *confession*, which simply means "to agree with."
We will never change unless we confess what is true
about our condition. Only when we confess that we are
stuck will we begin to work on getting unstuck. Only
then can we stop blaming others and excusing ourselves. We can then ask for forgiveness and receive it
(1 John 1:9).

2. *We have the ability to confess our failure to solve
our problems.* We are powerless to save ourselves. We
must come to a place where we say, "God, I have failed
in my attempts to change and to get better." We must
come to the end of ourselves.

We fail mostly because we try to overcome our
problems by "acts of the will" or by other self-improve-
ment methods. Yet any attempts to solve our problems
by ourselves will fail. "Therefore I will boast all the
more gladly about my weaknesses," wrote Paul, "so
that Christ's power may rest on me" (2 Cor. 12:9). Stop
trying harder. It will only bring you more failure.
Sometimes you have to stop trying and wait instead.

3. *We have the ability to ask for help from God and others.* This is the essence of *humility:* We recognize that we cannot do it alone. Maybe we can't change our sexual orientation, or stop spending money compulsively, or stop being depressed, or stop an eating disorder—but we can ask God and others for help. "Ask and it will be given to you" (Matt. 7:7). As James says, God is willing to help us: "You do not have because you do not ask God" (4:2).

4. *We have the ability to continue searching and asking God and others to reveal to us what is in our souls.* God's Spirit—and people—can help us to see ourselves as we really are. David asks God in Psalm 139 to show him what is wrong with him, and his request brings to the light the brokenness that needs to be loved, and sin that needs to be forgiven and turned from. In twelve-step language, this is the continuing "moral inventory." We grant God permission to change those aspects of us that need changing.

5. *We have the ability to turn from the evil that we discover inside ourselves.* In repentance we discover the sick, foul, and evil aspects of ourselves. Then we can say, "I do not want to side with that motive or part of me. I want to be different." When we are controlling, for example, we can confess it to others and to God. Then as we notice how we control others in our relationships, we can repent and turn from it. Character change comes as we confess our sin, get our real needs met, and repent from the evil that we find comes so naturally. We do not have to feed the evil aspects of our personality. We can begin to loosen our hold on them and let them go.

Don't think that this is easy. We enjoy our hatred, our bitterness, our envy. We enjoy lust and deceit. Yet realizing that these sins are ruining our lives can motivate us to give up whatever perverse pleasure we gain from holding on to these sins. We can allow God to meet that need in a healthy way through the love of him and his people. Giving up some evil aspects of ourselves and connecting instead to love is like trading in one friend for another. It is a death and a birth.

6. *We have the ability to find out what needs were not met when we grew up in our family, and then take those needs to the family of God, where they can be met.* God says that he "sets the lonely in families" (Ps. 68:6). Through God's family, his church, we can get our needs met. If we missed some necessary nurturing in childhood, for example, we can take our needy parts to others in the body of Christ and establish supportive connections. God asks the strong to meet these needs (Rom. 15:1).

If in childhood we lacked the training and support of a father, we can appeal to those in the body to help us learn and internalize what we did not get growing up. This is the "building up of [the body] in love" (Eph. 4:13 NASB). We cannot expect God to instantly and supernaturally heal the hurts people have inflicted on us. He heals through his people. Because our hurt comes from relationships, our healing must come from relationships also. Jesus asks his people to be his arms that wrap around each other. Our problem is that we seldom ask.

7. *We have the ability to seek out those whom we have injured and, when it is helpful, to apologize, admit our wrong, and ask them for forgiveness.* This is called making amends: "If therefore you are presenting your offering at the altar, and there remember that your brother has something against you, leave your offering there before the altar, and go your way; first be reconciled to your brother, and then come and present your offering" (Matt. 5:23–24 NASB).

The Bible teaches that to have peace with God, we must make peace with each other. We cannot claim to be right with God if we are not doing everything in our hearts to be right with others (1 John 4:20–21). A crucial aspect of getting well is purifying our relationships with other people and working hard on treating them well. This fulfills the second greatest commandment, "Love your neighbor as yourself" (Matt. 22:39).

8. *We have the ability to forgive others who have hurt us.* Having confessed our sins against God and others and having been forgiven, we can give that same grace to others (Eph. 4:32). In fact, our recovery and well-being is intimately tied to our forgiveness of others. It does us no good to receive grace with one hand and deal out judgment with the other (see Matt. 18:21–35).

We need to forgive not just with our will, but from the "heart" (Matt. 18:35), from our whole being. Forgiveness is a deeply emotional process whereby we deal with all our feelings. We must be honest about our hurt and anger and not close our hearts and become callous (Ps. 17:10; Eph. 4:19).

9. *We have the ability to develop gifts and talents God has given us.* He has given us abilities; we must use them. The difference between the "good and faithful servant" and the "wicked and lazy servant" in Matthew 25 is that the first one invested his talents. How much each servant accomplished didn't matter, but whether he had used what he received. The wicked servant did not even try to use what he had.

10. *We have the ability to continue seeking God.* God promises that if we seek him, we will find him; if we knock, he will open the door for us. He teaches us to persevere in prayer and in seeking the answer we want from him (James 4:2; Matt. 7:7–11; Luke 18:1–8).

11. *We have the ability to seek truth and wisdom.* Truth is God's revelation in the Bible and in his creation of how he and his universe works. We can be seekers of what he teaches in his Word and students of the works of his hands.

Wisdom is practical, applied knowledge, learned through living life. We must be intimately involved with living in the world and learning through experience (Heb. 5:14).

12. *We have the increasing ability to follow God's example of love.* Those who "love one another, as he commanded us" (1 John 3:23) recover. Those who hold on to hatred, revenge, and self-centeredness, do not. Love connects us with others, softens our hearts, decreases our isolation, and matures our soul. Practicing love is the best thing you can do to heal from emotional pain.

During my sessions with Jane, I discovered that she had dealt with depression for a number of years. Though she was a committed Christian, she never could overcome it. For years she had sought spiritual answers for her emotional pain. She tried giving it to the Lord, she memorized Scripture about her position in Christ, she prayed and meditated.

Finally, guilty and hopeless, Jane decided she was a spiritual failure. She became angry at God for his seemingly inactive role in her struggle. She had given her depression to him more times than she could remember. Why hadn't he healed it?

In counseling she learned that she had a lot of work to do. Having come from a very abusive family, Jane had developed a pattern of disconnecting from people. She did not allow herself to need anyone deeply, and her hurt was never touched by anyone. This pattern of isolation only renewed her depression every day.

As Jane worked hard to change her protective style of relating in individual and group therapy, she began taking responsibility for the work that *only she could do* in her sanctification process. She began telling her story to others and accepting their love and encouragement.

Jane did not change overnight; it took a long time. It

was hard, spiritual work—but not as she had previously understood "spiritual," that is, only prayer and Bible study. She learned to cry over her losses, to accept comfort from other people, to repent of the relational patterns that kept her from loving others. She learned to forgive those who had hurt her and to overcome her defenses that had kept her from responding to love.

To do all of these things, she also had to pray and study the Bible. Yet her prayer life took on new dimensions. She asked God to show her how she needed to change and to show her what she was hiding in her heart. She asked for courage to confront friends and family members, a task she had always avoided.

In short, Jane began to really "work out her salvation with fear and trembling." She learned that she could not merely "depend on the Lord" as some had taught her, but that he depended on her to possess what he had secured for her. She had to press on in the spiritual life.

With these changes, her depression lifted, and later she gave to others the comfort that she had received from God (2 Cor. 1:4). A wounded healer, she was able to love others and show them the new and abundant life God had given her. Only this time, Jane had done her part as well.

One day, I'll be finished with recovery.

Sal and Frances were elated. The Wednesday night Bible study they were hosting for the first time in their home was a success. They had team-taught a passage from Ephesians about relationships, and the four attending couples had participated enthusiastically in the discussions.

Frances usually kept her private thoughts and feelings to herself. Tonight, however, impressed with the warm, accepting atmosphere of the Bible study group, she decided to risk divulging something very personal during prayer-request time.

She took a deep breath. "I've been in therapy for a while to deal with a depression I've had since I was very young," Frances said. "The therapy seems to be working. I can see God's hand in my counseling. But it isn't always easy—the feelings are very painful. I'd appreciate prayer for God's grace in this journey."

Others mentioned their prayer requests. The group prayed and then broke for refreshments. Later, as people chatted together on their way out, Leonard asked Frances for a minute alone. They retired to a quiet corner.

"I don't want to sound intrusive," Leonard said, "but I thought perhaps I could help out with your prayer request."

"I didn't ask for anything but prayer," Frances said, surprised, "but I'm certainly open to help."

"I've seen this happen before in friends who have used psychology to heal their spiritual problems. They go on and on, session after session, and never really get better. It's a no-win situation, Frances. I wonder if it's time for the counseling to end. When do you really expect to stop being depressed? Perhaps a deadline would be helpful—you know, like, giving yourself another three weeks to stop being depressed."

Frances felt undone. Leonard's veiled accusations pierced her. She must not be doing something right, she thought guiltily, or she would have been finished with counseling by now, and over her depression.

When Will You Be Well?

Leonard's point has been made, in dozens of ways, by friends and families of Christians who are seeking help. They ask questions like these:
- Aren't you done with therapy yet?
- When will you be well?
- Isn't it getting worse instead of better?
- Isn't it time to get on with your life?
- Don't you need a deadline?
- Why don't you have a goal in mind?

At the heart of these questions is this crazymaker: "I will one day be finished with recovery." People who assume this idea think that spiritual growth is like changing a burned-out light bulb. Take the bad one out, pop the new one in. Problem solved. Life goes on. They think emotional struggles should be treated the same. Fix a depression. Cure a compulsive spending problem. Repair an anxiety attack. In any case, the process has a clear endpoint.

Some psychotherapists support this view. In any bookstore and from many mental health professionals, you can learn five-to-ten-session cures for emotional maladies. Most of them recommend a talk-to-yourself approach, such as "Start concentrating on positive things, and negative things like depression will go away," or "Learn proper financial habits so that you can say no to your spending impulses." When talking to herself doesn't work, the struggler begins to doubt herself (that is, question the healing process) and to distance herself from the healing agents the Lord may have sent.

Why Growth Doesn't Have to Stop

"So what's the problem with that?" you may ask. "I've heard horror stories about therapies that go on forever. Therapy has got to stop sometime, doesn't it?"

True. In fact, the Scriptures teach us that much in life does and should have an endpoint: "Desire realized is sweet to the soul" (Prov. 13:19 NASB). "There is a time for everything, and a season for every activity under heaven" (Eccl. 3:1). In his powerful, final written words, Paul proclaims the value of finishing: "I have fought the good fight, I have finished the race, I have kept the faith. Now there is in store for me the crown of righteousness, which the Lord, the righteous Judge, will award to me on that day" (2 Tim. 4:7–8).

God himself is a finisher. He created the universe in a finite period of time (Gen. 2:1–3). His work of reconciling us to himself he completed on the cross: "It is finished!" (John 19:30).

So, yes, it is true that whether we pray, study the Bible, see a therapist, or join a support group, we should expect results. A changed, healing life is the mark of the maturing Christian, just as the fruits of the Spirit are the signs of God's work in us (Gal. 5:22–24).

However, while we do successfully resolve problems such as depression, anxiety disorders, and compulsive behaviors, the sanctification process continues throughout life. We must be patient with ourselves and others while emotional problems are being worked on. We must also be patient in the face of our continuing sinfulness and immaturity—even when the psychological symptoms are over.

Yet those who cannot wait patiently for a struggler, those who tire of seeing a friend in therapy for month after month, those who wish their relative could conclude his recovery process and get on with life—these people are sidestepping crucial biblical truths about growth. When you believe that an individual will one day be finished with recovery, you bring on several serious problems.

Recovery and Spiritual Growth Are Split Apart

Those who teach this crazymaker misunderstand emotional recovery. Emotional recovery isn't removing a depression or curing a hot temper. Its roots go much deeper.

In his first recorded sermon, Jesus read from Isaiah 61:1–2: "The Spirit of the Lord is on me, because he has anointed me to preach good news to the poor. He has sent me to proclaim freedom for the prisoners and recovery of sight for the blind" (Luke 4:18). The word *recovery* implies finding or retrieving what was lost. It's an aggressive word, full of action.

In a nutshell, recovery means taking back what we lost in the Fall, recovering our place as God's image bearers, as stewards of the earth.

Emotionally, recovery means taking back character traits that we were robbed of: the ability to make deep emotional connections when we've been unable to, to confront evil in others when we've been afraid of conflict, to say good-bye to a perfect picture of ourselves and replacing it with God's loving acceptance of us, warts and all.

In other words, *recovery* describes the sanctification process, the spiritual-growth process, the task of reclaiming the image of God in ourselves, becoming like him (1 John 3:2). *Recovery* is another word for the maturing and healing events God accomplishes in our souls. We are using the term *recovery* in its broadest sense—not simply the clinical, emotional dimension.

You can't separate growth into "emotional growth" and "spiritual growth."

All growth is spiritual if it involves the biblical processes of love, responsibility, and forgiveness. All growth is spiritual if it produces a cheerful heart, concern for others, a deeper sense of responsibility, and an ability to set limits on evil.

In other words, Jesus was as concerned about the plight of the woman caught in adultery (emotional growth) as he was in the training of the Twelve (spiritual growth).

We Are Forced into Completing a Task, Not Growing

In college I was active in a Christian campus group, a ministry that emphasized Bible knowledge. We learned to read the Bible, study it, memorize it, and meditate on it.

I became a Scripture-memory addict. Memorizing Bible verses seemed like a practical way to get God's truth inside my head. So I memorized anywhere from two to ten verses a week. My goal was to memorize the entire New Testament in several years. The program was realistic, despite the fact that review sessions took an hour every day.

The larger problem was that I began hating the

Bible. I resented my schedule. I dreaded the reviews. I never wanted to see how far behind I was.

Looking for answers, I asked someone in my group how he coped with staying on schedule. He asked about my schedule, and I told him. "That's not how I do it," he said. "I memorize a lot fewer verses than you do. I try to get more mileage out of them. The way I figure it, I've got enough work to do with the few I already know."

I felt thirty pounds lighter. The advice helped me enjoy the Bible again, to look forward to spending time understanding and being helped by it.

Obviously, memorizing Scripture was not the culprit here. My own internal demand to finish the job was driving me crazy. I was more concerned with getting the verses memorized than being fed by the Word.

And that's the second problem with the "one day I will be finished" crazymaker. It focuses on the law, on completing the task, rather than on the journey, on how you get there. It distances Christians from the love of God and others, driving them anxiously toward the taskmaster of perfection. Arriving becomes the demand that breaks their backs.

The goal is love itself. Do you know Christians who know the Bible inside out, but are deficient in the ability to love? They haven't learned the lesson of 1 Timothy 1:5 (NASB): "The goal of our instruction is love from a pure heart and a good conscience and a sincere faith."

In fact, love is the process of achieving the goal as well as the goal itself. Learning to trust, to extend our heart, to take ownership over our resistance to love, is all part of God's recovery program. That's why people who get stuck on the question "When will I be finished?" miss the whole point.

It was during the 1960s that my hometown was shocked by the divorce of a prominent couple, both in their late fifties and active in the church. It didn't make sense. They were Christians, had raised three successful children, did well in business, and even went on mission trips. Their marriage seemed good. What happened?

Look at how their marriage was evaluated, though: a long track record of church involvement, kids who became responsible adults, the ability to build a successful business. Now look at how the marriage was *not* evaluated: How did they connect? What was their relationship like? What did they say and feel toward each other when they were alone? No one knew. In other words, the focus was on the goal, not on love. They had missed the central point of marriage.

In the same way, Martha was resentful that her sister, Mary, was lazily sitting at Jesus' feet, just being with him. "Lord," Martha complained, "don't you care that my sister has left me to do the work by myself? Tell her to help me!" (Luke 10:40).

Looking beyond Martha's jealousy, Jesus told her that intimacy was the better part, which "will not be taken away" from Mary (Luke 10:42). Mary's moments with Jesus would be a permanent part of her emotional memories, of her own character structure. They would make up a part of who she was for eternity.

People engaged in the recovery process learn to love the journey for what it is. They learn to stop and smell the roses, spiritually speaking.

"I was so impatient to be well, so I could get on with my life," a patient explained to me. "But my impatience made me resist entering the process. So I could never resolve my emotional issues. It was only when I realized that my goal orientation was keeping me from God and others, that things started changing."

We Lose Forgiveness

We are to heed the direction our lives are taking. Like a navigator plotting a ship's course toward maturity, we are to look constantly at our bearings and make adjustments. Throughout life we repeat the process: We get off target, make corrections, and get back on course.

Furthermore, it is impossible to be in this process without forgiveness.

Among my friends are several video-game fanatics who play in arcades, shopping centers, at home—anywhere. I used to try to compete with them. Now I just watch. I can't understand how they evade land mines, spaceships, and cannons for hours. Their eye-hand coordination astounds me.

You may remember the first time you played a video game. Your electronic maneuvering was probably clumsy, you overreacted to obstacles, you regularly dropped your animated character into pits.

If you persevered (unlike me), your character's actions became more subtle. You aimed, ran, kicked, and shot more accurately. You could consistently leap over the lava lake and avoid rolling monsters that spit flame. Young teenagers learning to drive steer with jerky overcorrections, yet they gradually smooth out their steering. But even professional drivers don't keep the steering wheel absolutely stationary. They're always adjusting, always correcting, always in motion.

That's what spiritual growth is like. We take a step, make a mistake, learn from it, and make a more educated step. We move from infancy to youth to adulthood (1 John 2:12–14). We blunder, confess, repent, and learn from our painful consequences.

And here is where forgiveness is everything: Since there's no condemnation in Christ Jesus, we are never alienated from love in all our overreactions and errors and outright sins.

For a few minutes, take forgiveness out of the picture. Suppose no cushion of grace catches us when we fall. Suppose that when we get off course, we face only condemnation and isolation. Suppose that as you played your video game, you failed to dodge the killer turtles. They get you—and enough voltage surges from the joystick and into your body to jolt you out of your chair.

You'd probably plot your next move very carefully, and give the killer turtles a wide berth instead of attacking them for extra points. You'd be in no mood to risk a mistake and earn another potent jolt of voltage. Your learning curve would be flat. Any video-champion potential in you would be destroyed. The cost of failure would simply be too high.

People who are told to ignore the process of recovery, who are told to get their lives together and simply decide to get well—these people are robbed of God's gift of forgiveness. They are given no room for trial and error, for risk and learning. There is no room for growth built on love.

Gene came to me for therapy about his depression. I learned that he had great difficulty confronting others, being direct, and taking initiative. In psychological terms, Gene was *aggressively conflicted.*

Every time someone at work took advantage of him, Gene felt angry, thought about saying something, then became violently sick to his stomach. When the nausea had passed, he was still too shaken up to try to resolve the conflict with the co-worker.

In Gene's childhood home, I discovered, any aggression on his part only met the violent rage of his alcoholic father. So he learned to sidestep issues, keep the peace, and walk on eggshells with his dad—and with the world.

Gene's aggression had been severely judged and wounded. In other words, when he wanted to tell the truth, his nausea stopped him—just as his dad had. His father had condemned Gene's aggression, and the nausea took over where his dad left off.

Gene needed a safe place to practice taking risks, a place where he could tell the truth without being attacked. He spent much time in a group doing this.

The first time he told a group member that he didn't like her interrupting him, the nausea rose in him as always, and he almost had to leave the room. The waves of nausea passed—and then the woman he'd confronted thanked him for his honesty. The more Gene practiced telling the truth, the more he was able to make mistakes, to take initiative, and to be more open. He'd moved from condemnation to forgiveness.

We Become Proud

A couple in my office argued about the husband's critical attitude toward his wife. Underneath a guise of concerned piety, he constantly belittled her about her lack of spiritual progress. She wilted under the sanctimonious barrage.

"Maybe it would help your wife listen to your statements," I suggested to him, "if you would tell us what your own spiritual weaknesses are—if you got the log out of your own eye first."

His face went blank. "Well, actually, I'm pretty much on top of it," he said. "My walk with the Lord is going well, and I'm meeting my spiritual goals."

"Then you're worse off than she is," I said. "If your biggest spiritual problem is her spiritual problem, your spiritual problem is pride."

My client was under the impression that walking with God meant staying out of trouble. Many like him imagine they can reach some magic level of maturity in which, as long as they keep turning the spiritual crank, all is well. Enough Bible study, prayer, worship, evangelism, and no apparent gross sin—and you have the classic "together" Christian. He had an ideal fantasy of himself as a Christian.

The only problem is that the Bible doesn't teach this. None of us will finish our spiritual journey in this life. We are all sinful, immature people who, no matter how much progress we've made, still need to agree with Paul that we are all sinners—"of whom," Paul wrote, "I am the worst" (1 Tim. 1:15). We haven't been made perfect (Phil. 3:12), and we won't be until we're with God.

If we believe that one day we will be finished, our tendency is to become proud and self-sufficient. We deny that we have much unfinished business, that we are beggars who need to daily cry out to God for the grace to help us with our problems, to test us, and to know our anxious thoughts (Ps. 139:23). Any teaching that leads us to think we've arrived at a final, satisfactory level of spirituality leads us out of God's arena and into Satan's.

The goal of spiritual and emotional growth isn't becoming perfect. The goal is a deepening awareness of ourselves, our weaknesses, our sins, and our needs. It is an increasingly clearer understanding of how much we need "so great a salvation" (Heb. 2:3 NASB).

Many Christians read in Matthew 5:48 Jesus' command to be perfect—and attempt to become just that. However, the Greek word *teleios,* translated "perfect" in many Bibles, is better understood to mean "complete" or "mature." Paul uses this word when he tells us, "All of us who are *teleios* [mature] should take such a view of things" (Phil. 3:15). God wants a grown-up, not a perfectionist.

Satan wants us to think like the Pharisee, not the tax collector (Luke 18:9–14). If we think we've arrived spiritually, we're no longer repentant, hungry, and needy—and we stop asking for help. And when we stop asking for help, we stop getting help (James 4:2). The squeaky wheel stops squeaking, then collapses without intervention from God and his resources.

We Despair

Finally, if we believe that one day we will be finished with recovery, we will sooner or later despair. If we're honest, we are acutely aware of our spiritual poverty. We understand that we'll never be ideal. And since the Bible seems to demand that we be perfect, we experience a loss of hope: "Hope deferred makes the heart sick" (Prov. 13:12).

Christians who are surprised by their regressions often despair. After having done well in recovery for a number of months, they begin again to eat compulsively, get depressed, or go into isolation.

A friend with a lifetime of emotional isolation went to therapy for depression. As he began working on his inability to attach to other people, he began to love others for the first time. Before his therapy, people had only been vague objects to him. He welcomed the change his heart was making.

Then a good friend of his was killed in an auto accident. Devastated, he raged against God for permitting the accident. The things he told God were so intense and graphic that they frightened him.

When he asked his Christian therapist about these intense, furious feelings, she told him that perhaps it was a sign that he wasn't saved.

"Maybe," I replied when he told me this. "But to me it's an indication that you *are* saved. You feel safe enough to confess to God what you are actually thinking. And you care enough about the relationship to tell him."

His therapist's reaction is shared by many Christians, who perceive regressions, feelings of rage, and failure as "backsliding" or "getting off track" or "going down the tubes." They do not understand that regression is built in to the sanctification process. If you were to chart the process of sanctification, you wouldn't use a straight, ascending line, but a zigzagging line, full of valleys and hills.

Failure and regression are normal. Uninterrupted success and lack of struggle are the exception. If Paul (by his own words) is the chief sinner, if Peter denied the Lord, if a murderer and adulterer named David is remembered as the man after God's own heart (1 Sam. 13:14)—if these are all true (and they are), then we must give up the idealized picture of ourselves, and allow our imperfect selves to be forgiven, loved, and matured.

Is There a Goal?

So what about progress and goals in the Christian life? Are we doomed to wander aimlessly, with the lackluster prospect of being unfinished seekers?

Absolutely not. Definable points of progress mark the path of spiritual and emotional growth. The mature person is one who has gained a level of proficiency or wisdom in the four developmental stages: bonding (the ability to give and receive love), boundaries (having a clear sense of responsibility), sorting out good and bad (the ability to receive and give forgiveness in a fallen world), and becoming an adult (being able to exercise adult authority in the world).

These marks of maturity indicate one who has moved, in the apostle Paul's words, from milk to meat, one who has learned to love and work wisely, who has come a long way on his or her spiritual journey.

Furthermore, we can also see progress in the reduction of clinical symptoms. Depression, anxiety, and compulsive behaviors follow the healing of the heart. They signal our spiritual and emotional condition.

Fevers drop only gradually. Cholesterol counts don't change overnight. And painful emotional symptoms resolve only gradually as one's spiritual condition changes.

People finish therapy successfully. They learn how to make emotional attachments. They develop boundaries. They begin accepting their own imperfections. Clinical symptoms begin disappearing. People generally no longer need professional help after successful treatment. But beware: Conflicts and internal problems are not over forever. As long as we're present on earth, we will have struggles.

And this means that we'll always need God's help and grace, the body of Christ, support groups, and intimate friends who know us inside and out. We'll always need to be soundly judging ourselves (Rom. 12:3). We'll always need to be growing.

As we mature, our cry to God should always be, "Be merciful to me, a sinner." Coming closer and closer to him exposes our sinfulness and neediness just as it exposes who he is. When we discover our sinfulness and God's majesty, we can go only in one direction: on our knees as Isaiah and Peter did (Isa. 6:1–7; Luke 5:8).

Learn not to ask the question, "Am I finished with recovery yet?" Learn to ask, "What's next on my journey, as I am known by God and others?" The endpoint—and the journey—is loving and being loved.

Leave the past behind.

I don't know how to begin," Jill said, looking troubled. "I'm afraid that if I tell you what happened, you'll think I'm an unfit mother or that I don't love my child."

"I don't know what it is you did," I replied, "but I can tell that you're very concerned about it. Why don't you tell me about it, and then we'll see what I think."

So Jill began. Whenever her four-year-old daughter made a mistake, such as spilling her milk or making a mess, Jill would lose control and explode. She would verbally attack her daughter, screaming horribly hurtful things and calling Amanda names. Then, devastated, she'd realize what she was doing and immediately leave the room. Her guilt overwhelmed her.

"How long has this been going on?" I asked.

"For about the last year and a half. Ever since Amanda became enough of a person to move around and make messes and mistakes. They're really not even mistakes; she's so young, I know she's just learning. But at those times, I totally lose control. I don't even think about what Amanda knows or doesn't know. I've lost it by then, and almost don't even know where I am."

"What have you tried so far?"

"Mostly memorizing Scripture about anger and taking 'timeouts' when I'm angry. But most of the time I can't do that. By the time I know I'm angry, it's all over."

"This may sound like a crazy question, Jill, but did you ever experience anything like that when you were a child?"

"Well, I ..." Unable to finish her sentence, she began sobbing uncontrollably. It was a while before she was able to talk again. When she did, she told horror stories about how her mother screamed at her, about how verbally abusive her home had been. Jill had only to commit some minor mistake, and her mother yelled at her that she was stupid, bad, worthless. Yet as she talked about her past, her pain and fear soon overcame her, and she soon shut down again.

She was reluctant to speak about her traumatic past, Jill said, because of what her pastor had taught her about looking at the past. "The Bible says that old things are passed away and all things are new," Jill told me. "I'm a new creation. How can things from the past have any hold on me? I must forget what lies behind and press on. I just need to depend on the Holy Spirit to empower me, and I need to repent of my anger, and I'm sure I'll be okay."

"Have you tried that?" I asked her.

Her look told me she had and that it had not worked.

She did not know why her past hurts were still causing her pain, and why she was repeating them with her own daughter. She felt helpless.

Jill's story is not unusual. Many adults repeat their parents' patterns in their own parenting, or are affected by what they suffered as a child. A thirty-five-year-old woman is unable to fall asleep at night because of memories of violence she suffered as a child. A happily married woman cannot have sexual intercourse with her husband because of memories of childhood sexual abuse. A forty-year-old man suffers immobilizing depression every time he watches his parents interact with his children, because he remembers how they raised him to be impossibly perfect.

In each instance, adults in favorable circumstances are being affected by things that happened in their past. Although they had tried to leave the past behind, those past events stubbornly kept disrupting their functioning in the present.

In these cases, people recognized how the past hurt their adult lives. Even more problematic, however, is when one's life isn't working—and the individual doesn't know why. He gets depressed or suffers panic attacks. She can't stop bingeing and purging. He spends his paycheck away as soon as he gets it. She is unable to meet simple goals she sets for herself.

The most common problems are relational: People are drawn into unhealthy relationships, or they constantly repeat a destructive relational pattern, regardless of their efforts to break it. For example, they find themselves attracted to critical or controlling people. Or they get hooked up with abusive individuals and are unable to repeatedly stand up to them. Or—and this may be the most heartbreaking—they are unable to respond to good people, distancing themselves from those who love them. And they can't figure out why they do it.

Some of them enter therapy, and their therapists reveal the connection of their problems to relationships in their past, or to past hurts that they've never dealt with. Such patients discover unfinished business inside them.

Then Christian friends or teachers tell them that because they are a new creation in Christ, the past should have no claim over them. They should "forget what lies behind and press on" (Phil. 3:13–14).

As if that's not confusing enough, some discover that it was therapy, not faith, that helped them deal with their past and that ushered them into a degree of freedom and resolution. Despite their increasing relief from emotional pain, they're nagged by guilt, by the feeling that they've done something unspiritual. After all, they reason, they didn't rely on Christ for healing, but ran off to therapy—what some Bible teachers denounce as humanistic, secular psychology. They feel as if Christ saved them, but therapy healed them.

In this chapter we will explore the false assumption *"I need to leave the past behind."* Proponents of this idea say the past is not important; we should just press on to what lies ahead. Yet this is a misapplication of Scripture; dealing with our past is very biblical.

The Nature of Your Past

Jason came into therapy because his wife was frustrated with his emotional distance from the children. As we explored what made it difficult for him to connect with his children, I asked Jason about his own father.

His father was wonderful, Jason told me, and he had always looked up to him. "It seems that you and your father did much better together than you and your children are doing," I said. "I wonder what went wrong."

"I don't know. Maybe it has something to do with his death."

"What do you mean?"

"He died when I was thirteen. He just never woke up one morning. I watched the paramedics come in and take him away under a sheet. Mom never talked about it. My uncle made all the funeral arrangements, but he didn't talk about it, either." And then he began to cry.

As we continued to work, he began to recognize his anger toward God for the sudden loss of his father, and toward his mother and uncle for not helping him through his feelings of grief. As he worked through the loss and felt the grief he never allowed himself to experience when he was a teenager, he stopped distancing himself from his own children.

His progress puzzled him. "Why did the past affect me now?" he asked.

"When were you feeling the pain of your father's death?"

"Well, now—today, as an adult."

"So, we really aren't talking about the past at all, are we? You carry your grief in your soul *today*. Your father's death occurred years ago, but your pain you feel today, right now. That is the present, not the past."

"I guess that's true," Jason replied. "I would feel distant every time I started to get close to the kids, because getting close to the kids got me close to my feelings about my father."

"I think you're right," I said. "The past can't really affect us, but our present feelings about the past can."

We as humans are caught in the flow of time. We divide our lives into past, present, and future. But the Bible looks at our lives from the perspective of eternity, in which there is no past or future—only the *present*. The things we would say are "in our past" are, according to the Bible, *part of our present*, since from the perspective of eternity that is all there is.

People have hurt us, we have hurt people, we have suffered wrong, and we have done things that are wrong. We would say, "All those things happened in the past and can't be changed." But the Bible shifts the focus from the past to the eternal present: "What is the state of your soul and everything in it *now*? Have your past experiences been exposed to the light? Have they been forgiven? Have you repented of them? Have you exposed the hurt to love and light? Have we grieved over and let go of hurtful things, or are we still hanging onto them? We need to see our lives and our souls not as past and present, but as eternal.

Again, what the Bible always asks of us is this: Have

the things in our souls—pain, patterns, skills, desires, fears—been exposed to the light of God's grace, truth, and forgiveness? If so, those things are healed and transformed. However, if we don't expose things of the past to the light of God's truth and love, they remain in darkness and are still alive *today*, creating fruits of darkness in us. Unconnected from the transforming power of God's love and light, they take on a life of their own.

Jill's relationship with her mother had never been brought out into the open, never been exposed to the light. Still plaguing Jill in a hurtful and unforgiving way, her relationship with her mother had not been transformed through forgiveness—and so it was very much alive in the present. Jason's grief for his father had never been expressed, so it remained alive, part of Jason's day-to-day feelings into his adulthood. Whatever in us has not been brought out into the open still has a life of its own in the past—and you can be sure that it will affect our present relationships.

The teaching that we need not worry about the past's influence on us is especially destructive and unbiblical because it forbids bringing the things that are in the darkness into the light and having the grace of God touch them.

A misinterpretation of the popular "forget the past" Scripture explains why many never bring their feelings into the light.

> But whatever was to my profit I now consider loss for the sake of Christ. What is more, I consider everything a loss compared to the surpassing greatness of knowing Christ Jesus my Lord, for whose sake I have lost all things. I consider them rubbish, that I may gain Christ and be found in him, not having a righteousness of my own that comes from the law, but that which is through faith in Christ—the righteousness that comes from God and is by faith. . . . But one

thing I do: Forgetting what is behind and straining toward what is ahead, I press on toward the goal to win the prize for which God has called me heavenward in Christ Jesus. (Phil. 3:7–9, 13–14)

"What is behind" Paul is not his hurts or situations that require him to forgive someone or even his old sins. The past that Paul is forgetting is his old way of trying to achieve righteousness. He spends the entire first part of this chapter listing his accomplishments to illustrate to the Philippians how he vainly tried to please God. But it didn't work, he says. He's leaving the old system behind. He's found a new faith.

In fact, by enumerating his accomplishments earlier in the chapter, he was bringing them to the light, confessing them, grieving them. He never denied what he had done.

Paul, then, is *not* saying in this passage to let bygones be bygones, as some inaccurately interpret it. To the contrary, the apostle models for us the act of bringing one's past to the light and confessing it.

Teachers who tell you simply to forget the past and press on are ignoring or even contradicting pivotal biblical commands. These directives reveal why dealing with the past is so important.

Expose the Deeds of Darkness

The first biblical directive is that we bring into the light whatever is in darkness. Our past, in biblical terms, is our history. The Bible isn't concerned about when something happened, whether today or ten years ago. The Bible is interested only in whether we have denied the problem and pushed it into the darkness, or whether we have exposed it to the light and dealt with it in God's way. Have we covered it up, or have we confessed it and brought it to the light?

Confession, or bringing things to the light, opens us up to the process of transformation. And transformation is what God is interested in: "Have nothing to do with the fruitless deeds of darkness, but rather expose them.... Everything exposed by the light becomes visible" (Eph. 5:11, 13).

We can see this truth in Jill's life. She was very angry at her mother for how she had been treated, and that anger had never been brought into the light. Hadn't her pastor told her to forget the past, like Paul taught? As a result, she had never been "angry without sinning," and that unresolved anger poisoned her relationship with her daughter (Eph. 4:26–27). By not dealing with her anger, she had given the Devil a foothold in her personality.

Besides covering up feelings and hurts from the past, we often have hidden motives generated by past relationships. For example, a man is highly ambitious in order to gain the approval of his mother. A woman approaches everything competitively, always thinking of coming out on top, in order to settle an old score with a sister. Such motives usually relate to a problem in a past relationship that has never been resolved.

In short, the past is important because, until we deal with it, it is part of what the Bible calls "the darkness" of our soul. If we have not confessed sins of the past or forgiven others for sinning against us, then these sins rule us, and the devil gains a stronghold in our lives. To teach that examining the past is wrong contradicts the Bible's teaching to deal with the darkness inside. Past relationships and feelings usually need to be dealt with in the present.

Forgive Everyone Who Sins Against You

Unless we look at the past, furthermore, we cannot truly forgive. Forgiveness deals with the past. Forgiveness is God's way of making right things that have hurt us. To know whom to forgive, we must know what happened to us, name the sin, and realize who is guilty.

The hurt and abuse people faced as children show themselves in behavioral and relational patterns—patterns that often result from unforgiveness in their hearts. Because they have never forgiven those who hurt them, they may still be unconsciously angry at them.

Tom constantly argued with his superiors over trivial matters. He made an issue of everything, then always had to get in the last blow. When he began exploring this problem in counseling, he realized that he was still trying to settle an old score with his father. His father always had to have the upper hand in a discussion and would put young Tom down whenever they talked. Although Tom thought he had forgiven his father years ago, his present behavior showed otherwise. He gradually realized that he had not forgiven his father, but was still trying to make all the authority figures in his life pay what his father owed.

As Tom got in touch with the anger he felt toward his father, he started to deal with the anger and let it go. That is, he began doing the work of grace: "Forgiving others as God in Christ has forgiven you" (Eph. 4:32). Once he accepted his father, he could accept other authority figures as well.

Heal the Brokenhearted

Another problem with teaching that you should leave the past behind is its disregard for the brokenhearted (much like teaching that Christians should not have pain, as we discussed in chapter 2). The Bible repeatedly describes how, in the words of the psalmist, God is "close to the brokenhearted and saves those who are crushed in spirit" (Ps. 34:18).

A primary way that God heals the brokenhearted is through his church. As its members, we are his hands to touch each other's pain. He has commanded us to love and minister to one another with compassion, mercy, confrontation, help, and strength. The New Testament repeatedly commands us to minister emotionally, spiritually, and physically to one another.

In fact, God gets plainly upset when his people do not help his hurting ones: "You have not strengthened the weak or healed the sick or bound up the injured." Not only will he do the job for us ("I will bind up the injured and strengthen the weak"), but he will destroy "the sleek and the strong," those with power who had fattened themselves by oppressing the weak (Ezek. 34:4, 16).

An individual may suffer pain now because of past wounds that have gone untouched by love. Such abandoned or otherwise hurt people carry broken, abused hearts. And however convincingly a teacher claims that such hurts simply vanish with time, they don't. They need to be touched.

What heals them is God's love through his people and his Spirit. When someone has a broken heart, they need the love of other believers. The Bible says that loving one another is a manifestation of the grace of God (1 Peter 4:8).

Those who have been hurt by the family they grew up in need the love and care of their new family, the family of God (Luke 8:21), to heal their old wounds and give them the love they need.

Grieve Your Losses

Openness to the past is the way through grief, which in turn is the process of letting go of things that we were once attached to. This letting go allows us to be open to the present. In short, loss opens the door to new life.

Grieving is a conscious process by which we deliberately release our attachment to persons, goals, wishes, or religious systems that we no longer can have. Our attachment to these outgrown things, in fact, keeps us from connecting to new and better things that God has for us (2 Cor. 6:11–13).

Lot's wife was one who held onto the past and was unable to connect with new things. Leave Sodom, God told her. But her ties were so strong that she was not able to leave completely. Instead of grieving her losses and moving on, she looked back longingly at her former life, and "she became a pillar of salt" (Gen. 19:26).

Jesus alluded to her when he taught the concept of losing one's life. "Remember Lot's wife!" he says. "Whoever tries to keep his life will lose it, and whoever loses his life will preserve it" (Luke 17:32–33). Ties to the old life keep us from living the new life God has planned for us.

Hurts and losses in our past can keep us stuck emotionally and spiritually if we do not grieve them, thereby releasing them. You can be tied to a person who is dead, tied to a person whose love you can't have, tied to the approval of someone who will never give it, tied to a fantasy impossible to realize. Whatever it is, an emotional tie to something from the past can keep us stuck in the present.

God's way of dealing with this is through grief, or letting go. We are freed by realizing what we have lost, feeling anger and sadness, and then letting go.

Listen to the value that the Bible places on grieving:

> It is better to go to the house of mourning than to go to a house of feasting, for death is the destiny of every man; the living should take this to heart. Sorrow is better than laughter, because a sad face is good for the heart. The heart of the wise is in the house of mourning, but the heart of fools is in the house of pleasure. (Eccl. 7:2–4)

Ironically, sadness can move a person out of pain and into happiness. Grief can transform a heart, a fact that many who have worked their way through depression can testify to. As they worked through their underlying sadness, their depression lifted.

Only when we feel the pain of our losses can we connect with the care available to us. "Blessed are those who mourn, for they will be comforted" (Matt. 5:4). Many have care available to them, but they are unable to accept it because they have not mourned. Grieving opens up a heart to let new love in.

Too many individuals experience a loss in life yet never grieve—despite the fact that it is normal to grieve. Scriptures record many instances of God grieving: He grieved the loss of a perfect creation. He expressed his pain and grief on the cross of Calvary. Jesus, a man "acquainted with grief," was sad when his friend Lazarus died. When we lose something important and do not grieve, our heart holds onto the old attachment—and we get stuck. We can move on only as the grieving process allows us to let go.

If our heart is frozen in grief, we are unable to feel feelings God has designed for us. Many people experience frozen grief as depression. Grief (sadness and anger) that has not been expressed and resolved leads to depression. (Solomon speaks of grief being associated with a happy heart.) Sadness and anger need to go somewhere. If we express them, we let go of them and can move toward happiness. But depression does not go anywhere; it sits like a block of mud. Often it needs to be washed away with tears of sadness, and then it moves out of one's system.

So avoid the teaching that one should leave the past behind, for it hinders people from grieving. If you do not grieve, you'll be stuck holding onto old things in your heart. Instead, do as Paul did when he "consider[ed] everything a loss" (Phil. 3:8). Talk about the past. Acknowledge it. Grieve over it, as God designed. (He gave you tear ducts for a reason.) Then let it go. Lose it. This death opens the door for a resurrection. Do not fear mourning, and pay no attention to anyone who tells you that mourning the past is unbiblical. "Blessed are those who mourn, for they shall be comforted" (Matt. 5:4).

Confess and Repent

When people examine the patterns they learned in the families they grew up in—that is, their families of origin—they are often accused of sidestepping their own problems and blaming their parents for their behavior. "Why do you avoid life?" they are asked. "Why do you insist on fixating on things you can't change?"

Certainly, it is easy to blame others when we ought to take responsibility for our own behavior. Some individuals are stuck in the blaming rut. (We addressed this problem in Assumption #4.)

However, there are solid biblical reasons for exploring the past—in particular, your past in your family of origin. We have already discussed some reasons: bringing things out of darkness, understanding whom we need to forgive, realizing with whom we should reconcile, and grieving.

An equally important reason for understanding the past is to repent—to turn away from patterns we learned in our families of origin.

The Old Testament records instance after instance of God confronting people for walking in the wicked ways of their fathers. He points out that they are repeating generational sin, and calls them to repentance. He gives them insight into their behavior.[1]

"Do not be like your fathers and brothers, who were unfaithful to the Lord, the God of their fathers, so that he made them an object of horror, as you see. Do not be stiff-necked, as your fathers were; submit to the Lord" (2 Chron. 30:7–8).

"Will you judge them? Will you judge them, son of man? Then confront them with the detestable practices of their fathers and say to them: 'This is what the Sovereign Lord says'" (Ezek. 20:4).

God asked them to see the evil of their fathers, disagree with it, and turn to his ways.

Nehemiah tells us that the Israelites "stood in their places and confessed their sins and the wickedness of their fathers" (9:2). We similarly experience spiritual revival and repentance by understanding which ways of our parents were not pleasing to God, were not ways in which he wants us to relate to him or to each other. Only when you bring these patterns into the open can you call them evil and turn from them.

Conversely, when people deny the sins of their fathers, they are destined to repeat them. If they never acknowledge hurtful, even evil patterns of relating, they blindly go on repeating them. They hurt their own children as they were hurt themselves.

Insight and confession, then, break the chain of generational sin and give hope. Yet many feel destined to continue dysfunctional patterns because they were taught an erroneous interpretation of Exodus 20:5, which speaks of sin being carried on into the third and fourth generations. That is a half truth, however. The Bible also teaches that God will honor any individual in a generational chain who repents; his repentance will help him break the links of that chain.

> The person who sins will die. The son will not bear the punishment for the father's iniquity, nor will the father bear the punishment for the son's iniquity; the righteousness of the righteous will be upon himself, and the wickedness of the wicked will be upon himself. But if the wicked man turns from all his sins

which he has committed and observes all My statutes and practices justice and righteousness, he shall surely live; he shall not die. All his transgressions which he has committed will not be remembered against him; because of his righteousness which he has practiced, he will live. (Ezek. 18:20–22 NASB)

God is always willing to forgive those who acknowledge their sin and repent. The chain of generational sin can be broken.

Much of repentance is looking at the past to see what you learned, from whom you learned it, and how you are repeating that pattern today. Confession and repentance of ungodly family ways—a common pattern—is a powerful dynamic of the spiritual life. Confess whatever wicked ways were learned in your early years, turn from them, and enjoy the freedom that comes from walking in the light of God and not repeating inherited patterns of darkness.

Personal Sin

If in this moral inventory we find not only generational, family sin but personal sin that we alone are responsible for, we need to confess that sin, ask for forgiveness, and move on (1 John 1:9). And this confession is not for God's ears only. We need to confess to each other (see James 5:16) in order to feel the full power of the grace of God. Many have never felt God's grace because they've never confessed their darkness to another person and felt his or her full acceptance. One of the ways we feel God's acceptance is through the love of his people (1 Peter 4:10).

In addition, we need to ask forgiveness of, and make amends to, the people we have hurt. Making amends leads to reconciliation, ownership of our sin, and help for the people we have hurt. Acknowledging our own sin against other people makes them feel better and helps them work through what we did to them.

Listen to what Jesus says about this:

> If therefore you are presenting your offering at the altar, and there remember that your brother has something against you, leave your offering there before the altar, and go your way; first be reconciled to your brother, and then come and present your offering. Make friends quickly with your opponent at law while you are with him on the way, in order that your opponent may not deliver you to the judge, and the judge to the officer, and you be thrown into prison. Truly I say to you, you shall not come out of there, until you have paid up the last cent. (Matt. 5:23–26 NASB)

God is serious about how we treat each other. In making amends there is healing for us as well as healing for those we hurt.

Changing the Past

It is blatantly wrong to teach that we should just forget the past, for the simple reason that the past will one day be our entire life. Past, present, and future are aspects of our soul that need to be reconciled to God.

We cannot change our past. But we must change our internal connections to those who have hurt us by forgiving them. We must release our demand that they somehow make it up to us. We need to let go of lost dreams and people.

We must take our living hurts from the past to those who can heal them. We must bring to light patterns we have learned from our parents and other adults, confess those destructive patterns, disagree with them, and repent from them. If we have wronged people, we must confess our sin, apologize to those we have hurt, and make amends.

Though none of these processes *change* the past, they nevertheless *redeem* the past. God is in the process of reconciling everything that has gone wrong, including our personal past: he deals with the past, reconciling people to himself, repairing damage, rebuilding what sin has destroyed. But in order for him to deal with our past, we need to bring all of our broken parts to him. This is the ultimate dealing with the past. God "was pleased to have all his fullness dwell in [Christ], and through him to reconcile to himself all things, whether things on earth or things in heaven, by making peace through his blood, shed on the cross" (Col. 1:19–20).

Bring your history to God, whether it happened two days or twenty years ago. Bring it to him and to his people, allow his light and grace to transform it, bring his truth to bear on it, and experience the reconciliation of your whole life.

If I have God,
I don't need people.

It had been more than two years since Roy and I had seen each other. Because he lived in another state, we didn't get together very often. So we had a lot of catching up to do during a quiet breakfast one morning.

But our lack of communication wasn't entirely due to geographical distance. There were things we needed to talk out.

Eighteen months earlier Roy had dropped off the face of the earth. A successful Christian businessman, he had been my friend for many years. One day he was fine, I'd been told. The next day he moved out of his home, took an apartment, and virtually disappeared.

For over a year Roy was out of contact with his friends and colleagues. He kept his job and visited his kids, but no one else ever saw him. He didn't return phone calls. Secretaries and answering machines ran interference for him.

His friends speculated about what had happened to Roy. Had he lost the faith? Had he gone crazy? Roy wasn't talking.

One night, out of the blue, Roy called me at my home and asked if we could get together. We made plans, and he flew in the next day.

Over breakfast Roy told me his story. For about a year he had been under extremely intense business pressure that required more of him than he had. He had tried to tough it out and be strong for others. "Times were tough," he told me. "I knew if my struggles were bad, others' had to be much worse." A deep depression followed.

Roy had shared his problem with only a few people. "Get some time away," one told him, "and rekindle with the Lord." "Do a personal inventory of yourself," another said. "Chances are, you've dropped your walk with God to a lower priority." A third told him, "God's rod and staff will comfort you."

So Roy began spending more time in the Bible and in prayer. Since stress and worry were waking him up at four A.M. anyway, he started using that time for his devotions. But his depression continued; black hopelessness and despair engulfed him.

His depression finally got the best of him. Roy's emotional pain became so intense that he oiled and loaded his revolver to prepare for the only solution he knew. But before he went ahead with his plan, he decided to move out for a few weeks to try to sort things out with the Lord.

One more shot at prayer. One more chance at an inspiring Bible study. Perhaps he hadn't really connected with God during the other attempts. Perhaps it would be different this time.

It wasn't. Roy prayed intently for hours on his knees. He read the Scriptures, poring over them to seek the Lord. And his depression grew.

"You're still with us," I said to Roy that morning. "What happened?"

"It was the strangest thing," he recalled. "As I was deciding to go ahead and end my life, my apartment neighbor knocked on my door to borrow a Phillips screwdriver. I got it for him, and we started talking.

"He wasn't a Christian, but he seemed interested. Bill let me talk and talk and talk. About my pain and life. About my insane business pressures. About my marriage struggles. About my abusive mother and my absent father. About my acting-out school years. About the brother who had let me down. About my conversion to Christ and how my life started coming around. About my many years of rescuing the world for God, and how the demands on me just kept growing.

"Bill listened and asked questions. He didn't offer advice. He told me he thought I had a really tough life. That was all. And after a couple of hours of my bending his ear, he asked if I'd like to go out to dinner. We did. And then he told his story."

Roy looked thoughtful. "It was the funniest thing. Bill didn't tell me to do anything. He sure wasn't God. He didn't say one word about God. And yet for some reason I felt better after talking to him than I did after talking to God. I hate the way that sounds, but it's true.

"I met some of Bill's friends. They were like him— people who had struggled, some believers, most not. But everyone seemed to want to listen to each other's problems. Nobody asked me to take care of them. Nobody asked me for spiritual advice. I could say whatever I felt, and they just accepted me.

"I felt guilty, because I wasn't around Christians. But I stopped wanting to kill myself. And strangely enough, I started wanting to pray again, which I'd pretty much given up on. Can you believe that? Feeling close to God with a bunch of nonbelievers!

"Anyway, after about a year, I started sensing more . . . substance, I'd guess you'd call it, inside me. And I knew I needed to get back to my family, my friends, and my life. So I'm home now. Everybody thinks I'm crazy, because I'm not talking much about it. But for some reason, I'm more ready to reenter life."

Roy leaned forward across the table. "Which leads me to why I wanted to talk to you. Why am I better? Why did hanging around a bunch of ordinary people help me? I believe God is sufficient for my needs. Yet it seems that he wasn't. So what's the deal? Is the Bible wrong? Isn't God enough for my needs?"

The "Me and God" Syndrome

Before we call Roy irresponsible, of little faith, or even crazy, let's look at his dilemma. Many Christians experience the same problem and ask the same questions.

In some ways, this crazymaker is easier to deal with than the false assumption we explored in chapter one ("It's selfish to have my needs met"). At least the "me and God" syndrome allows us to be in need. The problem is that it presents a biblically incomplete idea of how we get those needs met. Individuals who teach this crazymaker provide only part of the answer. It's a subbiblical view of how people get help.

The "me and God" syndrome says this: Since Christ is enough for me, it's me and God against the world. With God on my side, I can lick any problem. He's the pilot, and I'm the co-pilot in the battle of life. If he's there beside me, I need no one else.

In theological terms, this crazymaker is based on the doctrine of the sufficiency of Christ. Helpful when understood biblically, this tenet is based on passages such as Colossians 2:9–10: "For in Christ all the fullness of the Deity lives in bodily form, and you have been given fullness in Christ, who is the head over every power and authority."

Correctly understood, the sufficiency principle teaches that Christ provides for the believer's every need—physical, spiritual, and emotional.

The problem arises when we interpret Christ's sufficiency as Christ alone, not including his resources. We run into problems when we think that prayer and Bible reading are enough to keep us going, when we think that depression, loneliness, or anxiety can be solved by spending time alone with God.

This distorted teaching—"If I have God, I don't need people"—says that going to people for our spiritual or emotional needs is wrong. To those who ask for help from other people, teachers of this doctrine say:

- You lack faith.
- You have a limited, or small view of God.
- You are trusting in humans instead of the Savior.
- You are dabbling in secular humanism.
- You are in sin.
- You are proud.

And on and on. People who buy into this doctrine give testimonials to conquering depression, compulsive behaviors, and bad marriages because they turned from people and toward God.

So What's the Problem? God Is Sufficient, Isn't He?

God is God, you say, and he can do everything, right? Doesn't the Bible say God is sufficient? How can anything be wrong with this? How can this be a crazymaker?

God certainly is God, and God can do anything. Jesus declared that "with God all things are possible" (Matt. 19:26). He rules the universe (Rev. 19:6).

However, although he can, God doesn't do everything. God doesn't drive your car to church. He doesn't water your lawn (unless you live in Seattle). He doesn't tell your kids that you love them.

God uses all sorts of resources to help us in life. He uses angels as "ministering spirits, sent out to render service for the sake of those who will inherit salvation" (Heb. 1:14 NASB). He uses the witness of creation to draw us to him: "The heavens declare the glory of God; the skies proclaim the work of his hands" (Ps. 19:1). He used a donkey to talk to Balaam (Num. 22). And he uses people.

In short, God's love is manifested through many channels, including this one: his creatures loving and helping other of his creatures (1 Peter 4:8–10).

"Me and God" teachers say that God alone is the source of grace, of undeserved love. They say we shouldn't look to people for grace. Yet the Scriptures say that people are indeed a means of distributing God's grace to others: "We have different gifts, according to the grace given us" (Rom. 12:6); "But to each one of us grace has been given as Christ apportioned it" (Eph. 4:7).

If you're not receiving grace from God's people, your perception of God is too small. God wants to see love proliferate in his universe. That's what he is about, and that's what he wants us to be about.

God Uses People to Meet People's Needs

I was summoned to a psychiatric hospital to interview an emergency case for possible admission. When I arrived at the office, I met a distraught woman in her twenties.

When she was picked up in the middle of the night, Ruth had been walking down a country road, naked, and in a psychotic terror. The authorities called her parents, who called a Christian psychologist, who then called me.

As we talked, Ruth started to calm down. "What were you doing in the woods?" I asked her.

"I was on a spiritual-growth retreat."

"What kind?"

"To get alone with God for extended periods of

time, to journal what I'm learning from him, to grow closer to him."

"How extended is 'extended'?"

"A week. I stay alone every day in a cabin with my Bible and my notebook."

"You don't talk to anybody?"

"Once a day I have a session with my spiritual leader for an hour or so. We go over what I'm learning. Then I go back to my cabin."

"When did it get bad for you?"

"I got there on Monday. The first day or two were okay. But by Thursday I wasn't okay. At first I was just lonely, then I got really scared. By Friday, I thought I was being attacked by horrible beings, and I ran out of the cabin in the middle of the night to get away."

"What did your spiritual leader say about the bad days before the breakdown?"

Ruth paused for a moment. "He said that I was resisting the Spirit of God," she said. "He thought a few extra days might help."

The culprit here is not being alone with God, but that Ruth went into the retreat with an undiagnosed, severe abandonment panic disorder. It surfaced, predictably, as she became more and more isolated. Yet when she told her leader about it, his answer was for her to isolate herself even more.

This approach to spiritual issues is taught widely among Christian circles. It reminds me of the two tongue-in-cheek rules of engineering: (1) If it doesn't work, use a hammer; (2) if it still doesn't work, use a bigger hammer. Ruth's leader was using a bigger hammer on her, with disastrous results.

This is the first problem with the "If I have God, I don't need people" approach: It denies that God uses people as his fingers.

Yet God constantly uses people. We see people meeting other people's needs all the way through

Scripture. God looked at Eden and declared that it was not good that Adam had no human companion (Gen. 2:18). The Preacher says, "Two are better than one. . . . If one falls down, his friend can help him up" (Eccl. 4:9–10). And all the references to "one another" in the New Testament passages about the church (i.e., Rom. 12:10; 13:8; 14:13; 1 Cor. 12:25; 16:20; Gal. 5:13; Eph. 4:25, 32) point to this same idea: God meets our needs with people.[1]

Both-and, not either-or. Are you uncomfortable with the idea that God uses people? Does it make you feel that God never does anything directly through his Person or his Word—that he merely tosses people our way to represent him?

This is hardly the case. God isn't limited to people, but is highly and personally involved with us. He uses people for some things, and himself directly for others.

At a seminar on this topic, a studious fellow asked the question, "So what percentage of our needs are met by God and what percentage by people?"

We answered, "One hundred percent by both." As we'll see, it's actually God's hand behind it all.

Eyes and hands. God designed us to need each other in humility, so that we could relate to him as creatures to Creator. When we think we do not need what other Christians offer us emotionally and spiritually, the body of Christ stops functioning as it should: "The eye cannot say to the hand, 'I don't need you!' And the head cannot say to the feet, 'I don't need you!'" (1 Cor. 12:21). Needing each other's gifts, support, wisdom, and love is the biblical pattern for maturity.

There are four fundamental spiritual and emotional arenas in which God meets people where they are lacking: growth, comfort, wisdom, and repair.

1. *Growth.* Most Christians we know want to grow spiritually. Once the Father has drawn us to salvation in Christ, our hearts yearn to mature and become more of what we were intended to be—image bearers of him (Gen. 1:27).

One way this happens is through each other. As parts of Christ's body, the church (Eph. 1:22–23), we help grow each other up. None of us is complete. We have our crises and conflicts at different times and about different things. This way, when one is in need, he or she is helped. Paul explains it like this:

> Speaking the truth in love, we will in all things grow up into him who is the Head, that is, Christ. From him the whole body, joined and held together by every supporting ligament, grows and *builds itself up in love,* as each part does its work. (Eph. 4:15–16, emphasis mine)

"Builds itself up in love." Using the resources provided by God, we are to play a crucial part in each other's spiritual growth. Life in Christ is life in the body of Christ, his church.

Over the years I have belonged to several churches in which this principle is alive. The members helped each other when their babies were born, and they helped each other bury their dead. When anyone was in physical, financial, or emotional need, he called his spiritual family. Each part did its work, and the church grew in depth and breadth over the years.

2. *Comfort.* This is a basic spiritual and emotional need. We need someone to ease our pain, someone to soothe us when we're distressed.

One of the Hebrew words for comfort, *naham,* is rooted in the idea "to breathe deeply."[2]

To understand this, look how a mother calms a frightened infant. She holds him to her breast, next to her heart. The baby can hear his mother's heartbeat and deep, regular breathing. In a little while, his panic subsides, and he responds to the even, smooth functions of his mother. Comfort restores a sense of safety and order to us.

Comfort can come from God alone: "May your unfailing love be my comfort" (Ps. 119:76); "For the Lord comforts his people and will have compassion on his afflicted ones" (Isa. 49:13). The Holy Spirit comforts: The early church was built up and continued "in the comfort of the Holy Spirit" (Acts 9:31 NASB).

Roy's friend told the truth when he quoted Psalm 23: "Your rod and your staff, they comfort me." Yet he didn't go the next step and ask, "Can *I* help?"

People are intimately involved in God's comforting process. When Jacob thought his favorite son Joseph had died, "all his sons and daughters came to comfort him, but he refused to be comforted. 'No,' he said, 'in mourning will I go down to the grave to my son'" (Gen. 37:35). This important passage shows the healing power of the comfort of humans. Jacob refused the solace of his children because he knew it would promote the grieving process. Rather than resolve his grief, he wanted to somehow stay connected to his dead son.

"Trust God," advise some Christians to friends who experience loss. Yet these Christians are only condemning their friends to a lifetime of unresolved grief.

"People comfort" isn't just for those who have lost someone. When church members have sinned, then been disciplined for it, we should not leave them alone ("For his own good," we say to ourselves). Instead, "you ought to forgive and comfort him, so that he will not be overwhelmed by excessive sorrow" (2 Cor. 2:7). We should offer solace even if he deserved to suffer.

Paul had great joy and comfort in Philemon's love (Philem. 7). And when Paul was depressed, "God, who comforts the downcast, comforted us by the coming of

Titus" (2 Cor. 7:6). Job called his preachy friends "miserable comforters" (Job 16:2), who in the end were replaced by other friends and family, who "comforted and consoled him over all the trouble the Lord had brought upon him" (Job 42:11).

"People comfort" apparently comes in two kinds: good and miserable. It's helpful to study the comfort Job's friends offered him, so that you can duck when you see it coming.

If you go only to God for comfort, you may be limiting God's help. If we can't use his fingers, we're tying his hands.

3. *Wisdom.* In seminary we discussed endlessly what doctrinal camps we supported. Calvinism, Arminianism, pretrib, posttrib—we argued and analyzed for hours.

During one heated disagreement, one fellow made the mistake of asserting that he was no camp follower of anyone. He was, he said, a biblicist.

We roundly and relentlessly hooted him down for being presumptuous and arrogant. He said, in effect, "All the Bible scholars of the last two millennia are irrelevant. I understand the Word without their help."

We are to become mature in understanding the Bible. We're to aspire to handle the Word of truth correctly (2 Tim. 2:15). But we need the help of others to comprehend the Word.

Remember the Ethiopian eunuch's response to the apostle Philip, who had seen him reading Isaiah and who had asked the eunuch if he understood what he was reading? "How can I," the eunuch replied, "unless someone explains it to me?" (Acts 8:31). What if Philip had said, "Well, you need to lean on God to understand these words. See ya."

The point is simply that we all need wisdom—skill in living—whether it be in understanding Scripture, comprehending marriage, or figuring out depression.

And people are some of God's best resources in gaining this skill.

You'll hear the crazymakers, "Don't listen to people for your answers—get them directly from God." But do you see the implied contradiction? "Don't listen to what I'm saying, because I'm human."

So humbly consult "specialists" in whatever areas you need wisdom, whether it's about career, finances, anxiety disorders, or the will of God. Let God speak through those who have walked with him—and learn from them.

4. *Repair.* We all are broken in some way, both sinful and sinned against. Because none of us has escaped the results of sin, we suffer spiritual and emotional damage. We won't let others love us. We can't say no. We don't know how to connect with people. We're unable to be firm in our convictions. We need help to be disciplined, to accept our weaknesses, to stand against those who would abuse us. The broken, damaged, immature parts of our character need to be fixed.

As we said in chapter 5, the work of recovery is the work of sanctification. God is redeeming those lost parts of our souls that are injured. He is bringing those parts into the light of his grace and truth.

And doing this repair, many wrongly believe, is God himself, by himself, unaided by anyone or anything. All we really need, they insist, is to do what the Bible says.

Yet the Bible says over and over again that we should find people to help us return to spiritual and emotional health. The root meaning of the Hebrew word *hazaq*, "repair," is "to squeeze or bind." Among other things, it means "to help strengthen the hands and arms." The picture is of strong hands supporting weak ones.

In her old age a friend of mine was weak and frail, unable even to hold her fork to eat. At mealtimes I'd sometimes place my hand around hers, guiding the fork to her mouth. This *hazaq* brought us closer together.

It was this characteristic in the patriarch Job that Eliphaz saw and commended: "Think how you have instructed many, how you have strengthened feeble hands. Your words have supported those who stumbled; you have strengthened faltering knees" (Job 4:3–4). He was glad Job had *hazaq* (although Eliphaz neglected to give his friend any *hazaq* in return). Jonathan "hazaqed" David in a crisis: He "helped him find strength in God" (1 Sam. 23:16). It was through Jonathan that David received God's love.

The Bible doesn't dictate how God will meet a specific need—directly or through people. Yet we cannot assume a loving act of God over a loving act of people. God sent Titus to Paul (2 Cor. 7:6). God so loved the world that he sent his Son. Allow God to touch you through whatever or whomever he desires.

Don't Downplay the Incarnation

It was a difficult session for Carol. Her father had recently died after a lengthy illness. His death had been expected. What hadn't been expected was what she'd begun to discover about her relationship with him.

For a long time Carol had told me stories about the kind of man her father was. In all of them her father was loving, caring, strong, and protective. She had evaluated the men in her life by one standard—her father. There was only one problem: Carol's dad had left her and her mother when she was two, connecting with Carol only sporadically throughout her life.

So Carol had created in her head a perfect father. She'd embellished who he really was to protect herself from the pain and loss of not having had a father at home. Only after his physical death was she able to accept the death of the relationship several decades before. She began seeing her father for the real person he was—a troubled, self-absorbed man who really hadn't made time for her. She had a deep loss to work through—the loss of a man who had never been.

Carol never had a dad to connect with—one who held her, played with her, and took her on walks. Having no picture of a real dad, she fabricated an unrealistic one and compared every man she dated with this ideal dad.

The fact that Carol had a dad, somewhere, was not enough to save her from deep feelings of abandonment and loss. She needed a father in her house, a father in the flesh, a father incarnate. This only mirrors the need that God sensed within humans: In addition to the fact of God in our lives, we need God in the flesh, God incarnate—the Christ.

The crazymaker that says, "If you have God, you don't need people," distances us from the man Jesus. It minimizes the Incarnation, a fundamental Christian doctrine.

A fleshy religion. Most religions detail how to reach God. You perform certain rituals, you remain faithful to commands, you live the best life you can, or you recognize the god that you are.

In Christianity, however, we don't reach for God. We don't find the pathway to God. He reached for us, he made a path for us: "God was reconciling the world to himself in Christ, not counting men's sins against them" (2 Cor. 5:19). God saw that we were in deep trouble and would never be able to reconnect with him in his holiness. So he did the work for us: Christ paid for our sins on the cross.

In the Christian faith, God actually became man. That's what *incarnation* means. God became *carne*, flesh, for us.

By becoming a man, God baptized and affirmed our humanness. He made it acceptable to be just folks. We don't have to water down or transcend our humanity to be spiritual. To the contrary, to become spiritual, we must become more human.

By becoming a man, God showed that he understands our sufferings. He's been there. "For we do not have a high priest who is unable to sympathize with our weaknesses, but we have one who has been tempted in every way, just as we are—yet was without sin" (Heb. 4:15).

He became more thoroughly human than any of us can imagine: "God made him who had no sin to be sin for us, so that in him we might become the righteousness of God" (2 Cor. 5:21). The miracle of biblical Christianity is that the God-man wrapped himself in our sin until he paid for it. He took our sin upon himself and endured the punishment we deserved. Thus by a marvelous exchange he made it possible for us to receive his righteousness and be reconciled to God.

So if the flesh and bones and blood—and sin—of being human is apparently important enough to God that he became a man, then being human must not be all that bad. Furthermore, we can learn about love from the various ways the God-man loved people. He taught them. He healed them. He put his hands on them. He wept with them. He visited them in their homes. He even asked three of them to support him in his pain in Gethsemane: "My soul is overwhelmed with sorrow to the point of death. Stay here and keep watch with me" (Matt. 26:38).

This is how he met needs when he was on earth— with direct, hands-on compassion and love. The incarnation of Christ points out the absurdity of thinking you don't need people. When he was a man, God himself needed people.

This is what makes the sufficiency teachings insufficient. Proponents of this crazymaker teach a Christ who is definitely divine but scarcely human—contrary to the biblical teaching that Christ was fully God and fully man. They therefore limit the resources of Christ to God's direct intervention. They teach an insufficient Christ, not the Christ of the Bible.

The Gnostic split. At the root of sufficiency teaching is Gnosticism, an ancient philosophy that held that knowledge of spiritual things is essential. Matter—the opposite of spirit—is therefore evil. In other words, flesh is bad and spirit is good. The goal of a Gnostic, then, was to become less fleshly and more spiritual.

It was only logical that Gnostics treated their bodies, which were matter, harshly. Self-mutilation, deprivation, and isolation were commonly practiced by them, all to help Gnostics separate their flesh from their spirit. Their view of Christ? A purely spiritual Christ, not one tainted by humanity.

With the opening words of his first letter, John explodes this heresy:

> That which was from the beginning, which we have heard, which we have seen with our eyes, which we have looked at and our hands have touched—this we proclaim concerning the Word of life.

The apostle's point was that the Christ was also a man named Jesus, who lived, breathed, touched us, and died for us. In the same way he loved us, we are to love others. The spiritual Christian is very, very human.

For this reason, the phrase "body of Christ" is critically important. In passages like Romans 12, 1 Corinthians 12, and Ephesians 4 we read that the church operates as Jesus' body would if he were physically still on earth. We are to love each other, bear each other's burdens, and support each other. We are his fingers.

Learning about God. We learn about God's character from our human relationships. That's why the Bible says that "anyone who does not love his brother, whom he has seen, cannot love God, whom he has not seen" (1 John 4:20). People who are disconnected and estranged from each other have a more difficult time knowing and being close to God.

We see this continually in clinical practice, especially among Christians who can't sense any closeness to God after years of functional Gnosticism and sufficiency teachings. Only after they've worked on connecting to healthy people do they gradually begin sensing God more. They learn the spiritual truths only when the physical ones are in place.

Babies and spouses. It's almost impossible for "just me and God" teachers to live as they teach. If I am loved only directly by God, then for me to comfort others or help them grow would be to cause them to sin. I'd be teaching them to become dependent on people, instead of relying on God. Such a parent would have to stand over a crying infant's crib and tell her to be comforted by God—then walk away. Such a husband wouldn't kiss or hold his wife—he'd tell her that Christ loved her, and that's enough. The teaching breaks down in actual life.

In fact, the only way this system works is to stay away from people and simply point them to God. Yet that's exactly what James steers us away from:

> Suppose a brother or sister is without clothes and daily food. If one of you says to him, "Go, I wish you well; keep warm and well fed," but does nothing about his physical needs, what good is it? (James 2:15–16)

If they live what they believe, "just me and God" believers wish people well. Hoping God will take care of any unfortunates, they avoid helping them, in order that the needy will trust Christ even more. But that belief is a dead faith, James declares (2:17), and it needs to be buried.

God's Love, Shown through an Unbeliever

The actual tragedy in Roy's life, as he explained it to me during that long breakfast, was not his childhood sufferings (which were enormous) or his breakdown (which was traumatic). The tragedy was that there was no Christian for Roy to connect with. God had to bring an unbeliever to him. No doubt this circumstance was partly due to his resistance to Christians around him. Yet from what he told me, most Christians simply weren't available to be God's fingers. Instead they pointed the finger.

God made us to need him and each other. We need God. We need his Word. We need each other.

In his second letter, the apostle John wrote, "I have much to write to you, but I do not want to use paper and ink. Instead, I hope to visit you and talk with you face to face, so that our joy may be complete" (2 John 12). Complete your own joy. Come face to face with others who love you.

"Shoulds" are good.

I [Henry] grew up reading the Bible every day because I loved it. I had my own *Good News Bible*. From the fourth or fifth grade on through high school, I read my Bible every night.

When I got to college, I made a deeper commitment to God and joined a discipleship group that enforced a daily quiet time. Every week the group asked, "Are you having your quiet time?" I began to dread that question. Suddenly, when I didn't read the Bible and pray every day, I felt guilty.

Reading the Bible was something I had always loved doing. But when it become a requirement with negative consequences—when I felt had to do it or I would be condemned—I no longer wanted to do it. I moved from a world of "want to's" to a world of "shoulds."

In this chapter we will look at this supposedly Christian belief that can drive you crazy: "'*Shoulds*' are *good*." We will look at how we *feel* about duties we think we should do.

The word *should* expresses obligation, compulsion, duty. It implies that we have no choice; that if we do other than we should, we are bad or condemned.

Saying that shoulds that make us feel bad or condemned are *not* good is a difficult position to defend, for most of us have a deep sense of obligation.

We should fix dinner for our family. We should get to work on time. We should stop overeating. We should stop spending beyond our budget.

Then the shoulds invade our spiritual lives. We should set aside time for Bible study, serve on that board of directors, love our next-door neighbor who gossips. *The problem arises when we do things in order to be good, instead of because of the blessings we will gain by doing them.* The problem is doing good things from a sense of obligation instead of out of genuine love.

Our goal as Christians is to love the Lord our God with all our heart and with all our soul and with all our mind, and to love our neighbor as ourselves (Matt. 22:37–40). We cannot love unless we are free to *not* love—and see the consequences of both choices.

The underlying concept here is freedom. The traditional Christian concept of freedom is that we are free from specific ceremonial practices of the Mosaic law: We don't have to follow much of what the Old Testament commanded because Christ fulfilled those injunctions in New Testament times. However, real Christian freedom is more than just freedom from laws. It is freedom to choose life; freedom from fear, guilt, and condemnation when we make a wrong choice; freedom to choose love instead of avoiding guilt.

Freedom comes through grace. When we fail to be something we are not, or when we do something we shouldn't have done, we are truly free from condemnation through God's grace. We no longer *have to* do anything. Yet why do some Christians refuse to believe that they are free? What are the consequences of this thinking? And finally, what in particular is the joy of true freedom?

Why We Think We Are Not Free

Scripture often refers to the human race as slaves. They are owned by and absolutely subject to the will of someone else. They must obey—or else—whether the master is a person or an influence or a habit.

We are slaves to sin. "What I want to do I do not do," said Paul, "but what I hate I do" (Rom. 7:15). We seldom enjoy the destructive lives we often live; but we are "sold as a slave to sin" (v. 14). We get angry at our spouses. We overeat. We drink too much. We spend too much. We put things off. We criticize our neighbors. No matter how hard we try, we find that we have to agree with Paul. The good we want to do, we do not do—and we practice the very evil we hate. Why don't we do things that are good for us and that would make our lives better?

Because by nature, we are not free. We are slaves to the law of sin and death. As long as we are under the law, we will fail—as much as we try and as good as our intentions may be.

The person who trusts Christ as Savior is out from under the law of condemnation. She is "in Christ." This means that when God looks at her, he sees the righteousness of Jesus. Legally, she is not guilty (2 Cor. 5:21). No matter what she may be doing, she does not bear the legal guilt or condemnation, because Christ bore the guilt once for all. The consequence of sin for the Christian is never condemnation or punishment from God. The Christian is perfect in God's eyes because he is looking through the lens of Christ.

Experientially, however, we can be very much under the law. We can feel and act as if we will lose love if we sin. *Emotionally we are still under the law.* We feel that if we do not do as we should, we are bad or condemned and that we deserve to be punished. To the degree that we experience guilt, anger, and loss of love when we do not do as we should, we are still under the law.

When We're Under the Law ...

There are at least five major consequences of being under the law.

The Law Brings Wrath

The Bible says that the "law brings wrath" (Rom. 4:15)—first, the wrath of God. God is angry at offenses against him just as we get angry when someone hurts us. If we are under the shoulds of the law, then we expect God to be angry at us. Second, we get angry back at God. We resent him and his rules, and we want to move away from him. Third, we become angry at ourselves. Wrath is a natural fruit of the law.

Mary had struggled with her weight since she was twenty-five. At forty, she had gained and lost hundreds of pounds on every kind of diet you can imagine. She felt good when her weight was low, and angry when she fell off her diet. She would say vicious and angry things about herself, calling herself a string of brutal names. To her, the law—the emotional consequences of her failure—brought wrath more than it brought permanent weight loss.

We Are Condemned

When we are under the law, we are in a state of guilt and condemnation, subject to feeling guilty when we fail. We feel guilty, bad, or condemned if we do not do what we should.

Yet condemnation and guilt are not options for the Christian; only godly sorrow is (2 Cor. 7:8–11). Godly sorrow is sadness at having hurt God or someone else; it is focused outward on others. Godly sorrow produces change in us. Worldly sorrow is a feeling of badness; it is focused inward on ourselves. (Godly sorrow is distinguished from guilt, or worldly sorrow, more thoroughly in the next chapter.)

Because Rob had trouble reaching his financial goals for the family, he felt guilty. He made plans, but never did he stick to them. So he felt bad—but he didn't change. He became so overwhelmed with bad feelings that they paralyzed him, and he was unable to learn how to do better. Not until he dealt with his feelings of badness was he able to feel true remorse about the irresponsibility that led to his failures.

So if one feels bad or guilty or condemned about what he should do, he is emotionally and experientially under the law. If one feels sad or sorry about where he is, then he will be motivated to change. He is motivated by love. He will want to do better for himself and the ones he loves. Feeling guilty is "worldly sorrow" (2 Cor. 7:10); feeling sorry is godly sorrow, the key to true motivation. It is based not on wrath at self, but on love for others.

To unlearn our feelings of worldly sorrow, or guilt, is terribly difficult for most Christians to hear, not to mention to practice. Though they think that guilt is helpful, the Bible clearly teaches the opposite. Yes, we should feel sorry when we fail. That motivates us to change. But we should *never* feel guilt and condemnation. We have been freed from those so that we can get our minds off the badness of our inadequacies and onto the lovelessness of our behavior.

The writer of Hebrews says it this way: "How much more, then, will the blood of Christ, who through the eternal Spirit offered himself unblemished to God, cleanse our consciences from acts that lead to death, so that we may serve the living God!" (Heb. 9:14). We have been cleansed, "once for all by his own blood"

(v. 12), so that we are free from guilt to serve out of love.

We Are Separated from Love

Another consequence of living under the law emotionally is that it separates us from love. The law is hostile toward us. The law of God plainly says that the "soul who sins ... will die" (Ezek. 18:4). Death is separation from God. In other words, to be under the law implies that God does not love us, does not relate to us when we are *not as we should be*. If we do not do what we should, the law says, then God will not love us.

But the gospel says that God loves us whether or not we do what we should. In fact, it says that God loved us "while we were enemies," even before we were interested in doing as we should (Rom. 5:10).

Jim's life changed when he realized this truth. A pastor who had been trying for years to break free from compulsive sexual behavior, Jim finally came to the hospital for depression after he was caught soliciting a prostitute. He felt thoroughly unlovable and condemned. As he told his story to the group, he expected them, too, to condemn him because he had failed so miserably.

But he was amazed to find that his little group of recovering addicts accepted him exactly as he was. They did not withdraw love from him for his failure. They confronted him about how he had hurt his wife and family, but they never withdrew their love. Their acceptance proved to be the missing ingredient in his life and helped him get out from under the law and conquer his compulsive behavior. Finding out that he would not be hated when he failed changed his heart.

If we feel unloved when we do not do as we should, that means we are still under the law. Yet the New

Testament teaches that nothing we do can separate us from the love of Christ—we are totally loved as we are. We have "gained access by faith into this grace in which we now stand" (Rom. 5:2). This means that the love and grace of God is something that we stand in and cannot be removed from, no matter who we are or what we do.

We should never feel that we jeopardize God's love for us when we fail his expectations. Certainly, sin has other consequences we must face—but being separated from God's love is not one of them.

Sin Increases

The fact that sin increases when we're under the law is a confusing and destructive consequence. When we face something we need to do, we tell ourselves that we *should* do it. Yet the Bible says that when the shoulds become law, we'll sin even more. The instruction of Paul in Romans is clear about this: "The law was added so that the trespass might increase" (5:20), and "I found that the very commandment that was intended to bring life actually brought death. For sin, seizing the opportunity afforded by the commandment, deceived me, and through the commandment put me to death" (7:10–11).

In other words, Paul teaches that if we feel that the shoulds are laws with legal consequences, we will sin more, not less. The law will arouse within us the desire to sin more (Rom. 7:5). To our legalistic minds, this sounds like the opposite of what we suppose actually happens. Isn't it true that the more we tell ourselves we shouldn't do this or that, the more obedient we'll be?

If we feel we should do certain things because punishment awaits us if we don't, we have not died to the law (Rom. 7:4), and the law will have power over us. In other words, the very method by which we are trying to change will produce failure.

We are not saying that standards, which tell us what we should do, are bad. On the contrary, they are good. But if we think that we are condemned if we do not live up to the standards, we are still under the law in the legal and emotional sense, and sin will increase.

We Gain No Benefit

Whatever we do because we feel we should or because we have to is of no benefit. Our motivation is not love. Yet the reason behind all of the commandments, all of the "shoulds," is love. The shoulds have their place, of course, in this scheme of love: They are standards that tell us how we may better love God and others. But if we behave a certain way because we *should,* instead of because we *want to*, it profits us nothing.

Motivation is everything to God. If our motivation is compulsion or a feeling of obligation—a "should"—it is not love (2 Cor. 9:7). Paul would not even accept a gift unless it was "spontaneous and not forced" (Philem. 12–14).

> If I speak in the tongues of men and of angels, but have not love, I am only a resounding gong or a clanging cymbal. If I have the gift of prophecy and can fathom all mysteries and all knowledge, and if I have a faith that can move mountains, but have not love, I am nothing. If I give all I possess to the poor and surrender my body to the flames, but have not love, I gain nothing. (1 Cor. 13:1–3)

We may sacrifice in all sorts of ways that we should, but those actions can be meaningless unless we give because we love. If we do something only because we think we should—because we would feel unacceptable if we didn't—then we'd be better off saving our energy.

Because of these consequences, freedom from the shoulds is crucial. Only when we are free can we love freely. If we are in slavery to the shoulds because of guilt or fear, we are not ready to love. We must first be set free. Slaves do not love; sons and daughters do.

Freedom to Live

This sounds too much like license, some object. If we aren't condemned for what we do or who we are, why should we even bother trying to do the right thing? If we have total freedom, why not do whatever we want to do?

It's a natural objection to grace. Perhaps you feel yourself objecting to the total freedom we described above. We all have a strong legalistic streak that simply cannot let us believe what the Bible teaches about grace. We can't accept that grace is free and complete, and that we can't do anything to add to it in any way.

The Bible anticipated this reaction. "What shall we say, then?" Paul answers us. "Shall we go on sinning so that grace may increase? By no means! We died to sin; how can we live in it any longer?" (Rom. 6:1–2). The biblical response to total freedom is a refusal to live in death any longer. It is ridiculous to be freed only to want to return to jail. In verse four the apostle Paul says, "We were therefore buried with him through baptism into death in order that, just as Christ was raised from the dead through the glory of the Father, we too may live a new life."

For the first time we have a chance to be free from a life of death, and we have the opportunity to live a new life. We have been saved from what we are by nature— wickedness, evil, greed, envy, murder, strife, deceit, malice, gossip, slander, God-hating, insolence, arrogance, boasting, disobedience, senselessness, faithlessness, heartlessness, and ruthlessness (Rom. 1:29–30). And who wants this kind of life?

Still, the worried legalist in us asks, "But if the 'shoulds' will not keep us in line, what will?"

The Bible's answer is threefold. First, our love of God will keep us in line. The relationship and friendship we have with him is so great and empowering that it motivates us to be more like him and to not offend him. "God's kindness leads you toward repentance" (Rom. 2:4). We do not want to hurt someone we love (Eph. 4:30).

Second, our love and deep connected relationships within the body of Christ will keep us in line. When we love others and are connected to them, we don't want to hurt them, and our love for them constrains us. As the Bible says, "Do to others what you would have them do to you" (Matt. 7:12). Those relationships will also serve to discipline us. When we are out of line, other people whom we love and who love us will come to us in love and truth to tell us when we are wrong.

Third, we would be miserable living a life of sin (unless we are in denial). We usually recognize that the ways we live are not that satisfying. We get tired of our behavior patterns that cause problems in relationships, that set us back in life. When we finally figure out that the real problem is us, not everybody else, then we join Paul in thinking that we, too, may have a new life. We can have life, or we can have death. At any rate, we worry no longer about not doing as we should. Instead, we focus on the misery of our failed lives and the pain we have caused those we love.

The Bible offers no middle ground between the two options of life and death. Both are reality. Life consists of honesty, love, responsibility, forgiveness, fulfillment, and the like. Death consists of dynamics like deceit, separation, irresponsibility, judgmentalism, and unfulfillment. Paul puts it like this: "Those who live

according to the sinful nature have their minds set on
what that nature desires; but those who live in accord-
ance with the Spirit have their minds set on what the
Spirit desires. The mind of sinful man is death, but the
mind controlled by the Spirit is life and peace" (Rom.
8:5–6).

Finding the Deeper Life

At this point Christians enter the deeper life. They
have been Christians for a long time, but they've been
stuck. For years they have continued behaviors and
personality patterns they have tried often but vainly to
forsake and repent from. The chief reason for that
failure? They were living under the "shoulds." They
were motivated by fear, guilt, and feelings of badness.

There comes a time, however, when some Christians arrive at a state of genuine and shameless mourning. *It is here they want to change, not because they
know they ought to, but because they hate the hypoc-
risy, the lust, or the idolatry of their lives.* They are
dismal when they think what they're missing.

This is the beginning of what Jesus calls "poverty of
spirit," which brings them to grace in a much deeper
way than ever before. They find that they have to accept
the fact that though they cannot change, they are okay
in God's eyes as they are, and that he wants to help
them even in their badness, failure, and inability.

Then they begin to let others know them in that
state (James 5:16), they get their minds off the guilt and
the "try harder" cycle, and they begin to connect with
the love extended to them from God and others. They
also begin looking deeply at their own problems—and
that is when they begin to change. This is what has
come to be called *recovery.*

The true motivation that brings change is hating
one's life (Luke 14:26), then hungering and thirsting for

something better. "Blessed are those who hunger and thirst for righteousness, for they will be filled" (Matt. 5:6). This is very different from the guilt that comes from trying to do what we should out of fear and guilt. Guilt says, "I am so terrible." Love says, "I want to live."

Shoulds as Standards

Are shoulds good? Do they help us? The Bible's answer is a qualified yes (Rom. 3:31). The way that the Bible wants us to look at the shoulds is very different from the way we normally look at them.

Biblically, shoulds are what we need to do to live. Shoulds are the perfect law, our guide for life. They are reality. Doing what we should brings about a certain result, such as life and goodness. The Bible does not say, however, "You should, or else you're bad." It says, "You should, or else you will suffer and lose" (1 Cor. 3:15).

I finally came to understand this in college. I knew that if I wanted to live in a way that would bring life and goodness, I needed to read my Bible and pray. It would help me have the relationship with God that I wanted to have. But I learned that I would not lose the love of the Christian community if I did not read my Bible and pray everyday.

Shoulds are good in the sense that they are standards by which we see how we're doing. God's shoulds guide us on the way of life everlasting. They are the light on our path.

If we want to live, God's law is the way to life. As David says, "Open my eyes that I may see wonderful things in your law" and "Direct me in the path of your commands, for there I find delight" (Ps. 119:18, 35). In God's design, the law is intended to be a standard by which to evaluate ourselves.

God's shoulds help us to see where we need to grow, where we need to change. But when we see the discrepancy between who we are and who we need to be, we go to him for help in getting there. We do not crawl away from him in guilt because we haven't arrived yet spiritually, hiding and feeling bad because we are not doing what we should. The law is not judging us in a legal way, but guiding us in a loving way. It tells us what we need to do.

The Real Problem (and Solution)

When we do things because we think we should or we will be condemned, we are trying to do things right. But doing right is not the Christian answer, because doing wrong is not the problem. Doing wrong is only a symptom of the problem. The real problem is separation from God and each other.

Because we are born alienated from God, because we are separated from him and enemies with him (Rom. 5:10), we are hostile toward him (Rom. 8:7). We are cut off from him and do not have a relationship with him. When we are living apart from God, we are like dead people trying to be alive. Death, the Bible says, is not the end of life, but separation from God, the source of all life.

Salvation through Jesus Christ reverses this problem. Christ brings us back into relationship with God. We are reconciled to God (Rom. 5:10; 2 Cor. 5:18–21). We are connected to life again, and we produce the fruits of life instead of the fruits of death.

The essence of salvation is moving from being out of relationship with God into relationship with him, from being cut off from him and under the law of sin and death to being his heirs and receiving his grace. Decrees against us tell us what we *should* be like and what we *should* do, and when we are not being or doing

this, we are condemned. Even if we live a decent life
and fail in only a few points (which no one does), we
are still condemned (James 2:10). In salvation, however, there is no condemnation (Rom. 8:1).

A Life of Freedom

What does a life out from under the shoulds, out
from under the law and in relationship with God look
like? Let's look at two areas of life, relationships and
performance.

Love and Relationships

In relationships, being out from under the law
means that we are free to love. We do not *have to* love
God or anyone else (Josh. 24:15). We are free to love
whomever we please. But, looking in the mirror of
God's law, we realize that if we do not love, our lives
will be empty. We begin to see that a life without
fulfilling relationships is worthless, has little meaning,
and can even cause harm to others.

Being out from under the law means that I see my
failures to love as a serious problem, a cancer in my
soul. I do not grovel in guilt because I have cancer; I
am not condemned for my cancer. But I see it as a
serious problem for which I need immediate treatment,
or I will die. I become very sad and concerned about
my condition.

Being out from under the law also means I do not
put others under the law. They are free. I do not
condemn them, get angry at them, or withdraw my love
from them if they fail to love me in the way that I want.
So many marriages are legalistic, under the law. If one
partner fails, the other judges, condemns, and with-
draws love. The partners live out the essence of the

law, and it always produces death—in this case, the death of a relationship.

What do you do inside when your wife does not love you in the way that you want? In your perception of her, does she become bad? You are living under the legal shoulds when you conclude, "She should treat me in a certain way or she is bad." This attitude is judgmental and self-centered, and it never leads to resolution.

When we love people, we give them total freedom as God gives us. We accept them as God does us. They do not have to love us. When they fail to love us, or choose not to love us, we do not withdraw our love from them. We may confront them and make them aware of their failure. We may express our sadness about their choice. Sometimes we may have to invoke tough consequences. But we do not condemn.

Performance

When we evaluate our performance, we look at what we should be doing, but we do not condemn ourselves. When we fail, we own our failure. With grace, we do not need to be defensive, for we are not condemned.

Guilt says, "I should be different, and if I'm not, then I'm bad." Grace says, "I see the standard, and I'm not measuring up. I'm in trouble. I need to change if I'm going to live and have what I desire. If I want certain outcomes, I need to change." This is different from changing to avoid being bad.

When we live out from under the law, we begin looking at the *quality* of our obedience and stewardship. If in a realistic evaluation of them, we see they aren't up to standard, we are sorry. We realize that this is not how we want to be and we begin to seek God's help to change. In a phrase, we hunger and thirst for righteousness.

We are motivated to change because we want a different life for ourselves and for our loved ones, and out of love for God. Repentance works if it is motivated by a desire for something different, for something better than we have. Repentance merely to get the shoulds off our back always fails. To the contrary, prayer and Bible study aimed at finding God always work.

Compare two children, both of whom take piano lessons. One practices because his parents tell him he should and make him feel bad if he doesn't. When he moves away from home, he forgets music altogether. The other student practices because she wants to be a concert pianist. Her parents can't keep her away. This kind of motivation is lasting and is what every great doer has in his or her soul.

"Have to" Versus "Want to"

Coming out from under law means changing from "have to" to "want to." This does not mean that we always feel as if we want to do what is right. But it does generally mean that we want righteousness. Jesus did not want to go to the cross; but he wanted what it would give him: our salvation. In the same way, we may not want to do individual deeds of obedience, but we want the end result of our deeds. That is the true "want to." I want the end result, so I will do what I do not want to do in the immediate moment. Maturity expects delayed gratification.

The shoulds want us to "have to." We must or we are bad. We have no choice. Shoulds used in that way will always fail.

Be freed from shoulds, and you will start to live. You will be free to desire God and his life.

Guilt and shame are good for me.

W hatever Became of Guilt?" The sermon title in the church bulletin jumped out at Randy and Vicki as they sat in the pew. They looked at each other. Then, shrugging, they turned toward the pastor for the morning message.

The couple had been coming to this small, friendly Bible church in the Midwest since Randy's new job had brought them here from the West Coast three months ago. The warmth of the members encouraged them, and Pastor Glenn communicated the Bible message in a straightforward, no-nonsense fashion. It seemed that they had found a church home after their cross-country trek.

This Sunday morning Pastor Glenn came right to the point. "Beware of the humanistic approach to guilt," he preached. "A sense of guilt occurs because we're truly guilty. Listen to it. God provides guilt so that we'll know when we've missed the mark. If you *feel* guilty, you *are* guilty."

Randy and Vicki shifted uneasily. They weren't used to this approach to the gospel. Yet perhaps God was speaking to them.

"Guilt solves the problem of loving ourselves too much," continued Pastor Glenn. "Rather than concentrating on how wonderful we are, guilt refocuses us to the darker side. It puts who we are in perspective.

145

Focusing on guilt doesn't make us guilt-ridden. Instead, it makes us more responsible.

"The Holy Spirit speaks to us through guilt. Jesus taught about the conviction of the Holy Spirit in John 16:8: 'When he comes, he will convict the world of guilt in regard to sin and righteousness and judgment.' Don't quench him."

Driving home after church, Randy and Vicki were thoughtful. "Honey," he said, "I feel worse after the sermon than before."

Vicki nodded. "Same here. But maybe it means we need to get our act together."

"I didn't know our act *wasn't* together until fifteen minutes ago."

We Are Sinful, But . . .

"But what's wrong with that?" you may ask. "We *need* a sense of contriteness before the Lord. Don't at least the psalms teach as much, as in Psalm 51:17?"

We cannot deny that a sense of our sinfulness is biblical. Furthermore, it is common to feel worse *after* we encounter God—the prophet Isaiah and the apostle Peter both knew the feeling (Isa. 6:1–7; Luke 5:8). Awareness of our sin informs us of our need for God's forgiveness.

Pastor Glenn's message sounds Christian, but much of it is unbiblical. It burdens Christians with shame and guilt that God never intended.

Where's the Crazymaker?

This crazymaker states that guilt and shame are good for us, are helpful to our spiritual growth. Guilt and shame assist us by revealing our past sin to us—and they also prevent us from sinning again.

This false assumption is especially potent in those

who respect the Bible, because the Scriptures can be subtly twisted to teach guilt and shame messages. Families, for example, often use these messages to keep kids under control.

"Law is the easiest subject in the world to preach," my seminary professor used to say. "Grace is the hardest."[1] It's really not difficult to teach that—

1. The Bible says to obey God.
2. We don't.
3. We should.

Hundreds of Scriptures are preached that way. The only problem is, it doesn't help Christians grow spiritually. Most Christians already know they don't do what the Bible says to do, and that fact hasn't exactly set them free.

Pastor Glenn's sermon is an example of a theology of guilt and shame, which plays out in our lives like this:

- "You've ruined the party for all of us with your behavior. I can't show my face to my friends."
- "How can you be so selfish as to not lend me the money?"
- "After all I've done for you, you can't even come home for Christmas."
- "Shame on you for saying that to her!"
- "You really should visit them. They are your parents, you know."
- "There's plenty of people out there who need your help, and you're going on vacation?"
- "What am I supposed to do with myself if you can't go?"
- "You should have licked that eating disorder by now."

You get the idea. The speaker usually wants something from you and is angry that you aren't providing it.

The guilt message is simply a way to get you to change your mind.

Many Christians don't see the guilt trip laid on them in these messages. Trying to solve their guilt problem, they talk to themselves this way:

1. I feel guilty (due to my own conscience, to someone laying a guilt trip on me, or to both).
2. I assume I've sinned.
3. If I confess my sins, God will forgive me (1 John 1:9).
4. I confess, and feel less guilty.
5. I go on with my life until the next time someone makes me feel guilty.

The problem is that we can *feel* guilty without actually *being* guilty. And 1 John 1:9 isn't a bath for guilty feelings. It's a sin bath. We don't confess to get rid of guilt, but to have sin forgiven by God and to be reconnected in fellowship to him. There is much confusion about what the Scriptures actually teach about guilt and shame.

The Internal Condemnation of Guilt and Shame

Let's explore the concepts of guilt and shame first, then clear up the confusion surrounding them.

Guilt

Guilt has two common meanings: The state of having done a wrong (e.g., he is guilty of stealing the stereo) and a painful feeling of self-reproach resulting from a *belief* that we have done a wrong (e.g., he felt guilty for not coming home for Christmas).

On one hand, the Bible always refers to guilt as the state, not the feeling. You won't find Scriptures describing a feeling of guilt. The Bible describes a legal condition of guilt: "You have become guilty because of the blood you have shed" (Ezek. 22:4). "For all have sinned and fall short of the glory of God" (Rom. 3:23).

As a judge pronounces a defendant guilty, God has declared us legally guilty. We have missed God's mark of righteousness and need his solution, the Cross. By official pronouncement we are guilty for having broken the law.

On the other hand, *feelings* of guilt—as opposed to the *state* of guilt—are basically our consciences condemning us, telling us we're bad. Guilt *feelings* are painful, often causing us to criticize and condemn ourselves even more. Guilt *feelings* usually result from a sense that our actions have hurt someone. We may feel guilty about needing attachment to someone and consuming their time. Or we may feel guilty for disappointing someone, or setting a limit with them.

Some people feel guilty about letting others down through their imperfections or flaws. Olivia, for example, came to see me about a deep sense of guilt she bore over disappointing her husband. He was a talented musician. She wasn't. For years he had unrelentingly reminded her that her inabilities had limited his potential. He completely overlooked why he had married her in the first place; he never seemed to notice her many wonderful qualities. Olivia's grandiose sense of responsibility led her to feel that she had actually injured her husband.

Others may experience guilt when they show more talent or ability than another person. Still others feel guilty about simply existing, and taking up space on the planet. There is no end to the things about which we can feel guilty.

Shame

Shame is a painful feeling of having lost the respect of others because of our own improper behavior.

Though similar to guilt, shame has a broader definition in the Bible: It is both a state and a feeling. Shame can be a state of being despised by others (Joseph wanted to divorce his pregnant fiancée, Mary, quietly to avoid her being publicly shamed) or shame can be a feeling (Adam and Eve, in their pre-sinful condition, felt no shame). Shame is a *sense* of being bad, a state of internal condemnation.

Some people distinguish between the two words by saying that guilt describes our self-condemnation for *what we do*, while shame shames us for *who we are*. You feel guilty for yelling at your child; you feel shame for being a bad parent.

Of particular concern to us is the fact that guilt and shame both describe a state of internal condemnation, a pervasive sense of badness about the self, delivered by the conscience. These feelings can be mild or excruciatingly painful.

Guilt and shame arise from different sources. For example, some guilt is an awareness of our judged state—the fact that we are born under the law and severed from grace (Rom. 1:20, 2:14–15). Some shame comes from experiencing our own badness, as when "God chose the foolish things of the world to shame the wise; God chose the weak things of the world to shame the strong" (1 Cor. 1:27).

These types of guilt and shame are simply our emotional responses to the realities of our fallenness. They are good for us because they tell us that we desperately need grace, and they motivate us to look for help and forgiveness.

However, the guilt and shame that we are concerned with in this chapter come from a different source. They derive from early socialization processes. The conscience serves as an internal parent to monitor and evaluate the goodness or badness of our behavior. When the conscience approves, we feel relief. When it doesn't, we feel guilt and shame. This conscience-driven, environment-derived dynamic is what becomes a problem in spiritual growth.

Why Pastor Glenn's Message Was a Crazymaker

You probably remember the *Where's Waldo?* book series—cartoon scenes filled with hundreds of minute characters on the page, among which one was the bespectacled, stocking-capped Waldo. The challenge was to find him among the hordes of sunbathers, farmers, trolls, firefighters, animals, and the like.

Welcome to "Where's the Crazymaker?" In the Sunday message Randy and Vicki heard lie the major theological errors of the "guilt and shame are good for me" false assumption. Now that we understand the true natures of guilt and shame, let's take a biblical look at Pastor Glenn's message.

Pastor Glenn Deified the Conscience

Pastor Glenn claimed that *feeling* guilty is a sign that you *are* guilty. Guilt feelings, he said, are an emotional red light that tells you that you have sinned. God speaks through guilt and shame. So listen to them.

Ken exemplified this thinking. A highly self-critical professional man, he came to the hospital program for severe depression. Ken loved people, but his excessive sense of responsibility contributed to an unrelenting guilt problem.

I observed the climax of Ken's problem in group therapy one morning. For the first few minutes, everyone was quiet. Some members mulled over the work done in previous group sessions. Others were just timid about initiating conversation in a group setting.

Detained by a medical workup, Ken came in a few minutes late. He took his seat. Several people smiled at him, and the group stayed quiet a few moments more.

Ken gradually became more and more agitated. I watched him squirm restlessly in his chair, rubbing his hands together and perspiring. Finally he could stand it no longer. "I'm sorry! I'm really sorry!" he blurted out.

The group members asked him what he was apologizing for.

"I ruined the group," he said shamefacedly. "I know why the group is so quiet. I disrupted you all by being late, and now no one wants to talk. I'm really sorry!"

Ken's conscience was punishing him for being late. He assumed that his conscience's judgment was accurate. He assumed that he had disrupted the group session. But he hadn't.

Many Christians feel the same enslavement to a shameful conscience Ken did. But we don't have to. Let's look at a biblical view of the conscience.

The first thing we notice is that our conscience is a product of the Fall. Human beings didn't always have a conscience. Adam and Eve didn't have one, because they didn't need one. They had a direct, uninterrupted connection with God.

In addition, Adam and Eve were never intended to deal with issues of morality. Questions of good and evil weren't meant for humans, but only for God. God knew that if we had knowledge of good and evil, we would turn our focus from relationship to rules, from love to legalism. Being good would become more important than being connected.

That's why the only tree whose fruit Adam and Eve were prohibited from eating was the Tree of Knowledge of Good and Evil (Gen. 2:9, 17). And when they ate, God said, "The man has now become like one of us, knowing good and evil" (Gen. 3:22). Adam and Eve now had knowledge of good and bad, but without the character strength of God to deal with it. They were banished from the Garden.

The banishment was actually an act of mercy. God ejected the first couple so that he could later work out the problem of sin through his Son. Otherwise, they would have remained eternally hidden from God in the Garden. So humankind was stuck—out of the Garden, out of perfect connection with God.

At this point conscience began. It occurred as a product of our loss of relationship with him, as we began responding to the internal law of sin and death (Rom. 8:2). It was an adaptation, of sorts, to learning how to sort out good and evil. The conscience became an "evaluator," refereeing the goodness and badness of our thoughts, actions, and feelings.

Our conscience isn't God. It's part of living in a fallen world, and in a judged state. This internal referee combines the law written on our hearts by God (Rom. 2:15) with our early socialization processes. But it isn't perfect.

For example, people with overstrict, guilt-laden values will feel excruciating guilt when they are innocent. In contrast, people raised with no sense of right and wrong will feel no remorse when they should.

The Bible describes three types of conscience: the weak conscience, the seared conscience, and the mature conscience.

The weak (or immature) conscience. The weak conscience is an overstrict, punitive internal judge that finds guilt everywhere. It takes responsibility for much more than God intended, as Ken did.

Paul describes the weak conscience like this: "Some people are still so accustomed to idols that when they eat such food they think of it as having been sacrificed to an idol, and since their conscience is weak, it is defiled" (1 Cor. 8:7). In other words, the weak or immature conscience prohibits, criticizes, and accuses unjustly.

The seared conscience. A seared conscience is the opposite of a weak conscience. The person with a seared conscience has little sense of remorse. The sociopathic personality has a seared conscience; he can't feel empathy for the suffering of others. He lives by the law of the jungle: Eat or be eaten.

Those with seared consciences generally come from families in which they suffered such terrible abuse that they live in a state of perpetual rage. Or they come from families with little structure or love. With no attachments and no limits, people become small gods to themselves.

Those with seared consciences become controllers or manipulators of others. Paul warns Timothy against "hypocritical liars, whose consciences have been seared as with a hot iron. They forbid people to marry and order them to abstain from certain foods" (1 Tim. 4:2–3).

The mature conscience. Over time, the mature conscience is able to more and more closely approximate biblical values as it makes judgments. When the Bible speaks of a "clear conscience" (Acts 24:16; Heb. 13:18; 1 Peter 3:16), it indicates a person using a scripturally trained internal monitor. To have a clear conscience doesn't mean you're perfect, but only that your conscience is accurately helping you make biblical judgments about your actions.

As a product of the image of God as well as a part of the Fall, our consciences change and grow with us. As we help the conscience mature, we can trust it more.

But it is certainly fallible. Equating the conscience with God makes as much sense as equating a cult leader with Jesus Christ.

Pastor Glenn Confused Guilt Feelings with Godly Sorrow

The second crazymaking point Vicki and Randy's pastor made is that we need to focus on guilt. Certainly, a sense of our sinfulness is necessary for repentance; but Pastor Glenn described something very different from that.

Guilt feelings focus on our badness. They focus on our feelings of worthlessness and our deserved punishment. They are essentially self-absorbed, not other-centered. Guilt moves us not toward relationship, but into hiding.

Godly sorrow is a better response to our sinfulness:

> Yet now I am happy not because you were made sorry, but because your sorrow led you to repentance. For you became sorrowful as God intended and so were not harmed in any way by us. *Godly sorrow* brings repentance that leads to salvation and leaves no regret, but *worldly sorrow* brings death. See what this godly sorrow has produced in you: what earnestness, what eagerness to clear yourselves, what indignation, what alarm, what longing, what concern, what readiness to see justice done. (2 Cor. 7:9–11, italics mine)

Here Paul teaches the difference between godly sorrow (remorse) and worldly sorrow (guilt). Godly sorrow is empathic, centering on the hurt we cause to someone we love. We feel bad because we feel the pain of the person we've injured.

We are destructive. We hurt God: "I have been hurt by their adulterous hearts which turned away from Me" (Ezek. 6:9 NASB). We hurt each other: "Their mouths are full of cursing and bitterness. Their feet are swift to shed blood; ruin and misery mark their ways" (Rom. 3:14–16). We constantly cause pain to those we love.

Godly remorse seeks to heal, to make restitution to those we've hurt. Reconciliation and relationship are its goals. To the contrary, guilt seeks self-justification. It attempts to get rid of the bad feelings.

Judas displayed worldly sorrow, or guilt. When he felt remorse, he tried to return the thirty silver coins to the priests and elders. He was more concerned with his misdeeds than with restoring his relationship with Jesus. The fruit of his worldly sorrow was suicide (Matt. 27:3–5).

The next time you miss the mark, search your emotional response. If it centers on how bad you are, your emotions are the sorrow of the world. But if your response centers on loving your neighbor as yourself, it is likely to be the sorrow of God.

Unlike godly sorrow, guilt holds us back from two highly desirable objects.

First, *guilt prevents love.* Those who are preoccupied with their guilt may look loving; but when you try to talk to them, they are absorbed with their own pain. They work harder trying to get rid of their own guilt feelings more than they work at feeling the pain of others.

When a husband tells his wife (as one I know did), "I'm staying married to you because I couldn't stand the guilt if I left," there should be no mystery why she cannot warm up to him. Such a husband is more concerned with not feeling bad than with nurturing his wife.

Guilt-motivated people are afraid to love. They give of themselves under compulsion rather than cheerfully (2 Cor. 9:7). They do loving things to avoid feeling guilty, not because they want to.

Consider the following scenario: You make plans for

a weekend trip with a good friend. Two weeks before the trip, you call your friend to confirm your mutual plans. She tells you, "Oh, don't worry—I would never forget this trip. If I did, I'd just hate myself. Being responsible to my friends is very important to me. I don't like letting them down."

Her comments probably wouldn't affirm you as a desirable friend. She is obviously more concerned about avoiding guilt than she is with spending time with you. Yet this is the attitude that runs unspoken in the head of many guilt-ridden individuals. Love just doesn't have room. Love's want-to is smothered under guilt's ought-to.

Second, *guilt prevents spiritual and emotional growth.* People don't make genuine progress emotionally until they conquer their guilt feelings. There are several reasons for this.

Guilt-ridden people are afraid of being themselves because they fear further condemnation. So they generally adopt false selves that appear to be getting better, while they bury their wounded selves deep inside. This is common among Christian circles where a guilt message is taught: The compulsive or depressed person starts acting happier to keep the helpers happy. After a while, however, she breaks down—a process the helpers interpret as "backsliding." In reality, her wounded soul had all along stayed hidden, and the problem had multiplied inside like a cancer.

Guilt-ridden people are emotionally under the law. They are not truthful about their weaknesses because they fear they will lose love. Admitting failure, they fear, will bring condemnation and isolation from God and others. People who are constantly frustrated in their attempts to be perfect begin seething inside— they can't fulfill the law, can't please their guilty consciences. It's futile. The fruit of those attempts is only rage (Rom. 4:15).

Guilty people are more concerned about being good and sin-free (an impossibility in itself) than about getting well. They focus on the questions, Am I being good? Am I sinning? Am I bad? instead of on the questions, Am I connected deeply to others? Am I being truthful? Am I learning from my mistakes? When we focus on being good, we move into self-absorption and a compulsion to keep the rules—and we move away from closeness, intimacy, and relationship with God and others. You don't open up to someone you think is holding a baseball bat over your head.

Pastor Glenn Confused Conviction with Guilt

Leaving church one morning, I overheard a comment between two friends. "I really felt the conviction of the Spirit during the sermon," one said. "I feel so guilty now that it's just got to be God."

This comment typifies the third problem in the message Randy and Vicki heard that Sunday morning. Although their pastor referred to John 16:8 as evoking guilt feelings, he did not understand the difference between God's job and ours.

When Jesus said that the Holy Spirit would convict the world of guilt, he was describing the Spirit's role in salvation. The Holy Spirit exposes our sinfulness and need for a savior. But he doesn't dictate our response. Guilt, godly sorrow, rebellion, or indifference aren't from him; they come from us.

The churchgoer whose comment I overheard should have said, "I'll have to think about whether my guilt is a response to God or to my critical mother."

Is Guilt Ever Good?

One good thing about guilt feelings: They can be a sign of spiritual growth. Many who are recovering from emotional problems have severe guilt attacks. Leaving the old ways and cleaving to new ideas and people activates their controlling consciences—which then rain down "You're being bad" messages to stop the mutiny of biblical freedom. Such consciences are saying no to your freedom. A critical conscience wants to keep you a slave to its mandates. It wants you to obey its idea of goodness, not the Bible's.

If you're in recovery and beginning to address your true spiritual needs for attachment, responsibility, and forgiveness—and you're getting beat up by your conscience—rejoice! You're probably doing something right. Then find friends who will help you work through the feelings.

What Can You Do?

If you're motivated by guilt or shame, you cannot also be motivated by love. A strict, guilt-inducing conscience is not from God. Ask him for help in finding people who can move you from guilt and shame to love, and follow these steps:

1. Own the guilt. It may have been built into you by too-strict relationships, but it's now your problem, and you can do something about it.

2. Get into a support system that is more concerned with relationships than "sin-busting," a group that understands that "God's kindness leads you toward repentance" (Rom. 2:14).

3. Investigate where you learned the guilt messages.

4. Become aware of your anger.

5. Forgive whoever controlled you.

6. Learn new information to reeducate your conscience, from the Scriptures and from books like this.

7. Internalize new voices from your support group. Guilt isn't resolved by simply retraining your mind. You need to replace critical voices with accepting ones.

8. Don't resist grief. Let others comfort and love you through the process.

"This then is how we know that we belong to the truth, and how we set our hearts at rest in his presence whenever our hearts condemn us. For God is greater than our hearts, and he knows everything" (1 John 3:19–20).

If I make right choices, I will grow spiritually.

As Laura listened to the sermon on Sunday morning, she grew more and more depressed. Discouraged about so many areas of her life, she had come to church searching for hope.

Here she was, thirty-one, and back again in another hurtful romantic relationship. Laura felt helpless to stand up to her boyfriend, who in a critical and downright mean way manipulated, dominated, and generally controlled Laura's life. Every time she decided to confront him, she backed down.

Furthermore, she was sleeping with him, even though she felt bad about it. She had been told many times that men who pushed you to violate your values were not men with whom you could sustain a long-term relationship. But, somehow, she never found the willpower to say no.

Laura was weak-willed in other areas of her life as well. A yo-yo dieter, she tried again and again to eat right and exercise, but never could follow through. Nor could she stand up to her mother, who still tried to control her life. She knew that she must live her own life, but could not find the willpower to resist her mother's manipulation.

On this particular Sunday, Laura had gone to church yearning for some help. The pastor ended his sermon by saying, "It all comes down to choices. People choose to do what they want to do. If you really want to serve God and live a spiritual life, you will. You will stop sinning, and make right choices. By an act of the will, you will choose God's ways over your own. Go out from here today and make right choices."

Laura's heart sank. She had heard it all before. She had tried to make right choices for years. But try as she might, she could not find within herself the willpower to make the choices she knew she needed to make. If this was all that God had for her, she really *was* without hope. She slipped out of church and glumly drove over to her boyfriend's house. At least she would not be alone.

"Just Say No!" advised the popular drug-education program. The sponsors thought that just saying no was the answer to the drug problem. Other people have held the same philosophy about other problems— anger, lust, depression, addictions. If we have problems, they say, we're merely making wrong choices. What we need to do to correct the situation, they say, is to understand what the right choices are, then make them.

If you truly believe this, life becomes pretty simple. All you need to know is what is right, and then do it. *Knowledge* and *willpower* become the tools of spiritual growth. The cause of spiritual growth, then, is making right choices.

It sounds Christian. Indeed, the Bible has much to say about choice. Joshua encouraged the Israelites to choose: "If serving the Lord seems undesirable to you, then choose for yourselves this day whom you will serve, whether the gods your forefathers served beyond the river, or the gods of the Amorites, in whose land you are living. But as for me and my household, we will serve the Lord" (Josh. 24:15).

Certainly we have no problem with Joshua's laying

out the choices. We do need to choose whom we will serve—and that choice has eternal significance. The problem, as we saw in False Assumption #8, is that the spiritual life is not that simple. Spiritual growth, or sanctification, does not end the day we choose God. Yes, we can choose God—but we can at the same moment constantly sabotage our own "choice." That is, we choose the exact opposite of what we have committed to.

This happens frequently in daily life. You choose to diet, but three months later you are twenty pounds heavier. You choose to stay calm, yet you go berserk when your spouse gives away the punch line of your joke. You choose to be sexually pure, yet you can't help sleeping around. You choose to have a consistent prayer time, but you can't get up in the morning.

"Just Say No" has failed because the doctrine that willpower is the answer is a human doctrine, not a biblical one. *Willpower fails.* With the best intentions we choose one thing (as an act of the will) and then do the opposite. Instead of just saying no, we experience what the apostle Paul did: "I do not understand what I do. For what I want to do I do not do, but what I hate I do" (Rom. 7:15).

So this crazymaker says, *"If I make right choices, I will grow spiritually."* If making right choices is our only hope, then we are indeed hopeless. Paul's experience and our own reveal our inability to just say no.

Why Doesn't It Work?

Why doesn't making right choices work? It sounds so spiritual, so Christian. Why isn't it biblical to choose our way to health? Why can't we grow by an act of our will?

Many Christians teach that if we can change our behavior, our feelings will follow. Act lovingly toward someone we hate, we're told, then we will begin genuinely to like him or her. Choose what is right— whether you feel like it or not—and you will inevitably begin to desire that right thing.

It works that way sometimes. What happens more often than not, however, is that a person's initial commitment to do what is right is undercut, and then she is back where she started—or worse.

The undercutting often occurs as what has come to be known as compulsive behaviors. If someone is caught in a compulsive cycle of acting out sexually, overeating, taking drugs, or drinking excessively, he may choose to stop, but he inevitably falls into the same cycle—despite commitments to God, himself, and others to stop.

Ike was a pastor caught up in a cycle of sexual acting out. He preached sermons about purity one night and engaged in illicit sex the next. When his board of elders found out, they gave him an ultimatum: Begin intensive counseling, or resign.

At first, Ike talked a lot about how sorry he was and how bad he felt about his behavior. He made commitments to change, promising never do it again. And then the group confronted him.

"I don't believe that you'll change at all," said a group member. "I think that you will just act out again and again."

"But this time I really mean it," Ike said. "I *will* do it this time. I just made some bad choices."

"What makes you think you won't make them again?"

"Well, because this time, I'm really serious about wanting to change. I'm really committed."

"Weren't you 'really serious' all the other times? You always felt bad about what happened, and promised to change. But that never does it. *And if you don't do something other than choosing to change, why should we believe that it will be any different this time?"*

Ike looked depressed. He was beginning to see that he would repeat the same cycle if he did not do something different. But he did not know what to do. He was hopeless. He saw no options other than trying to make a stronger commitment in the future.

What was wrong with Ike? Why didn't his efforts and commitments work? What he began to realize was that, although he wanted to change, he wanted other things just as deeply, things he had denied. These desires were deep in his heart, where motivation arises. He strongly desired to be accepted and admired—a desire that wasn't being met within his congregation. He wanted to hurt his wife because he resented her criticism about his haphazard way of handling household finances. He wanted to rebel against the spiritual obligations he had taken on and now resented. All of these motives produced destructive fruit in his life.

In short, Ike's heart didn't respond to his "act of his will" theology, primarily because, in his understanding of his will, there was no place for his heart. *The Bible makes it clear that the will is not separate from the rest of the person.* We do things with our entire person, not just our will, or intellect. The greatest commandment reveals this fact to us: "Love the Lord your God with all your heart and with all your soul and with all your mind" (Matt. 22:37). Jesus paints a picture of an integrated person who takes all of himself—not just his conscious will—to God.

Ike lacked integration. He chose with his will to stop acting out sexually, but with his heart he chose to continue. Unless we will as a whole person, our minds and our hearts willing the same thing, our choices are short-lived because we end up doing what our heart chooses. We are divided on the inside. God confronts this split: "These people honor me with their lips, but their hearts are far from me" (Matt. 15:8). If we fail to own the conflict, the disowned part of us will sabotage our choice.

Ike eventually learned to confess to God and others what was actually in his heart. When he was honest, he found he had conflicting desires. He had never faced how dark his heart really was. He admitted that a part of him really did not want to serve God at all. He resented God. He had a lot of pain and grief that he had never faced, and he was trying to cover up that pain by acting out sexually. His true self was not in relationship with God or others at all. And so this self had a life of its own; it willed him into an entirely different direction than where his intellect told him to go.

Internal Conflict

Our mind, soul, and heart are often in conflict with one another, and we do not like to face conflict within ourselves. We may know what is right and what our values are; but in our hearts are deep loves and affections for things and people that are contrary to our values. For this reason, the Bible always calls for change from the inside out, not just making right choices.

Stan had a problem obeying his boss. He wanted to do well in his work, but inevitably he would sabotage his own best intentions. He met with his boss for planning sessions, where they reviewed Stan's goals. He initially looked forward to meeting those goals— after all, he was paid extra for good performance—yet shortly after these first few meetings, he began procrastinating and not fulfilling his commitments. He simply didn't get the job done.

So he came to see me. "I don't know why I do this," he told me. "I really want to do what I am supposed to. I just need to make better choices."

"What do you mean by 'better choices'?" I asked him.

"Choices that please God and get me where I want to go. Choices that accomplish what I want to accomplish."

"What makes you think you aren't doing that now?"

"What do you mean? Of course I'm not accomplishing what I want to accomplish."

"I'm not so sure. Maybe there are things you want to accomplish other than achieving your and the company's goals."

"Like what? My behavior is ruining my career."

"Yes, it is," I said. "But maybe your career is not the most important thing to you. I think something else is much more important to you than achieving your business goals."

"Like what?"

"You are much more interested in feeling like you are in control of yourself; no one is going to have power over you. In a work situation you feel one-down to your boss, and you resent that. So you resist doing what he wants you to do so that, even though you fail, you are in charge.

"Basically you hate authority so much that you can't exercise any in your own life. And it is hurting you very much. But the pattern is also keeping you from feeling some very old feelings that you have never resolved about being one-down to power figures. So what you have never really recognized and owned is that thwarting authority figures is a much more important goal to you than making money. Your head knows that to do the right thing would help you, but in your heart is still so much hatred for authority, that your heart overrules your values. Until you deal with that conflict, you will continue to win by losing."

Stan had no idea how to deal with his conflicting feelings and wishes. Ever since adolescence he had been in conflict with authority figures. On the outside he was a "good" boy, agreeing to do what those in authority wanted because he wanted their approval. But he disappointed them with his ultimate performance. He had so fooled himself into believing that he wanted to please his father and other authority figures that he had gotten out of touch with his conflicting feelings about them. As a result, he complied on the outside, but was determined on the inside not to be controlled. The inside always won.

"A good tree cannot bear bad fruit, and a bad tree cannot bear good fruit" (Matt. 7:18). As hard as the bad tree tries to bear good fruit, it cannot. This is what can happen to Christians who try to choose good fruit, but have not faced the bad aspects of their heart. Jesus gave a better answer than the "make right choices" model; he called for *character* change: "Make a tree good and its fruit will be good, or make a tree bad and its fruit will be bad, for a tree is recognized by its fruit. . . . The good man brings good things out of the good stored up in him, and the evil man brings evil things out of the evil stored up in him" (Matt. 12:33, 35).

Internal character dictates what we ultimately choose to do. *If we have problems in our heart, no amount of trying to make right choices will produce good fruit in us.* We must deal with the things that are on the inside and driving our choices.

Stan needed to deal with the deeply conflicting motives in his heart. He needed to confess his hatred for his father and for other authority figures. He needed to forgive them, to own his sin of rebellion, to seek forgiveness, to find care and affirmation from other Christians to fill the empty place inside that his father had never filled. He needed to face his sadness about what he had always wanted and never gotten from his father.

And he needed to face his fears of failure, to step out

and try new things. Avoiding responsibility had kept alive his fantasy that he really knew more than all his bosses; procrastinators can never be proven wrong or inferior to doers, because they can sit back and passively criticize. Stan had to take chances and occasionally fail—a painful process in which his pride had to die.

How Then Do We Grow?

If making right choices cannot ensure spiritual growth in us, then how do we grow? *First of all, realize that choice is necessary but not sufficient for growth.* Spiritual growth is always a combination of choosing the good, gaining the support and strength to do it, and dealing with the bad.

So equally important to our choices is submitting ourselves to God and to his church for support and absorbing his Word and his truth. Through relationships we forge in the body of Christ, we must confess the deep aspects of our heart. We must learn to depend on God's Spirit to discover what is choking our spiritual growth. We must dig around inside the root system of the tree to remove what is choking its growth. And then we must practice what we are learning (Heb. 5:14).

The Bible calls for painful surgery. Resolving again and again what you will do is easier than submitting to the knife that cuts into your deepest motives and feelings, and exposing them. Deluding yourself into thinking you will change *this* time only delays the pain of actual transformation. If we do not change on the inside, we do not change at all. No magic act of the will transforms character.

Bad Out, Good In

Spiritual growth is both cultivating the good and weeding out the bad. To make right choices, most of us do one or the other—cultivate the good *or* weed out the bad. We usually work only on one side.

To the contrary, the Bible says we must take care of both sides of the problem. Only then will we be able to sustain good choices. We must add what good things we need *as well as* uncover the bad things—both internal and external—and turn from them.

People who try to stop eating, for example, will fail precisely because they deal with only one side. Without food, they feel the isolation driving their lust for food. They try to say no to the bad (overeating) without replacing it with something good (deep relationship with people that would end the isolation).

When people say no to drugs, they begin feeling the pain that they tried to cover up with the drugs. When they stop acting out sexually, they get depressed because they have to face the inner emptiness and pain that was driving the sexual behavior. If all they do is make the right choice—to stop the behavior—they leave themselves in misery. They are unable to sustain the choice simply because the driving motivation is still there. The need drives the lust.

The Bible confirms that when we stop sinful behavior, we begin to suffer (1 Peter 4:1–2). When we stop living after lust, we will suffer in the flesh. People experience the underlying pain when they stop acting out their addictions.

The apostle Peter says that "since Christ suffered in his body, arm yourselves also with the same attitude" (1 Peter 4:1). We need to prepare for the suffering to come when we stop bad behavior. Yet God does not leave us there. He wants us to fill the needs that are driving the lusts. He wants to provide for us through the grace of his people. He does not want us to give up one thing without replacing it with another.

Sally was forever getting into destructive relationships with men. She made poor choices about romantic relationships. Each time, her friends told her to to leave her current boyfriend; she usually agreed wholeheartedly that it was the right thing to do.

But when it came down to it, she never could make that choice. She always felt so horrible after breaking up that she could not sustain it. The depression would override her will. Her "act of the will" wouldn't act. And soon she was back in similarly hurtful situations.

Sally is an example of destructive behavior patterns, whether about relationships, eating, or drugs. She attempted to say no to the bad, but she did not deal with the entire picture. Not only did she need to say no to the destructive choice of going back, she had to face the absence of the good within her as well. She did not have the love she needed to ward off the depression she felt when she broke off a relationship.

In her soul, in fact, Sally had a lot of empty places — a perilous situation, Jesus reminded his listeners once with a story about a person who got rid of the bad within (a demon), and yet he did not further clean out his house and fill it with good things. So when the demon returned, the house was still unoccupied. The demon found some friends and took up residence again, and things were worse than before (Matt. 12:43–45).

There was no place for love and truth within her, that the Bible says we need in order to survive.

For Sally to conquer her pattern of choosing destructive relationships, she had to do some work inside: Grieve deeply over past pain that she was seeking to alleviate in these relationships, confess old anger that she was acting out in these relationships, take some good things into her soul to ensure that she would choose good in the future. She needed God's truth and the loving connection of other people.

In the past she would soon feel so empty again after a breakup, that her resolve evaporated and she ran back to the man she had left. Yet she finally took responsibility for her emptiness, saw a therapist, and got into a good support group. She began to feel other people's care. By taking in some good, she was able to say no to the bad. And this time she was able to sustain it. No inner strength is why codependents (including those addicted to substances) get better only with a support group.

Right Versus Pure Intentions

A *right* intention is the choice to do the right thing. We choose the proper, God-pleasing thing to do, and usually take little account of whether or not we *want* to do it. We just do it. Many evangelicals base their theology on this old-fashioned "act of the will" thinking. The key to spiritual growth and success, they insist, is to know the moral code and follow it.

We saw earlier that people who have right intentions, who choose to do the right thing but whose heart isn't in it, are often far from God's will. They can choose to do the loving thing but gain nothing (1 Cor. 13:3).

A *pure* intention is wanting what we choose. In the biblical sense this is what it truly means "to will." The words most often translated "to will" actually mean "to desire." *For this reason, to think of an act of the will apart from a pure heart that desires the things God desires is unbiblical.* God wants us to will and want the same things that he wants.

But we do not desire what God desires without having our heart changed. We need to take the deeper desires of our heart—lust, envy, resentment, hatred, revenge—to God for him to transform. Conflicting motives sabotage our lives and produce bad fruit. But as we take those evil desires to God and to others in the body of Christ, we find that they are transformed through confession, grace, and repentance. As we receive from him, we gradually find that our character begins to want and desire what he wants and desires. And then the "right choice" is not nearly such a conflict between what we want and what we tell ourselves we *ought* to want. We begin to will the things that he wills. We not only choose to treat others lovingly, but we want to.

Through a combination of "work[ing] out [our] salvation with fear and trembling" and a "God who works in [us]," we begin to be transformed—and then we come into line with his "good purpose" that he is working out in us (Phil. 2:12–13). In the process of acquiring pure intentions (instead of *right* intentions), we begin to hunger and thirst for righteousness (Matt. 5:6).

Spiritual Growth Leads to Right Choices

We saw early in this chapter how right choices are often held up as the *cause* of spiritual growth. But we have seen that making right choices is a *result* of spiritual growth. The ability to make right choices is a fruit of the Spirit (Gal. 5:22).

When our theology tells us we can make the right choices, we know we're being prideful. We are unable to save ourselves, Jesus said—unable to do the right thing. He told us to own the fact that we are poor in spirit, which means we are unable to do what is right. To admit this is humility—which is simply surrendering our assumption that we can make right choices. We admit our spiritual poverty (Matt. 5:3), recognize that we can neither save ourselves (Matt. 16:25) nor be perfected through the power of the will or human effort (Gal. 3:3). God must transform us.

Since we cannot make the choices we want to make, what choices can we make? We can choose to—

- Confess our sins
- Give up the notion that we can save ourselves
- Submit our inability to God
- Ask for help in searching for our faults
- Repent
- Take account of our needs and let others meet them
- Make amends
- Forgive
- Invest and practice talents
- Seek God
- Seek truth
- Love one another

All these choices assume weakness and humility. They focus not on being good, but on working out problems. These choices will succeed, where trying to be good will fail. These choices are based on our sinfulness and inadequacy, not on our goodness or ability to make godly choices. These choices will produce spiritual growth that bears the fruit of self-control and the ability to make right choices.

Therefore, instead of trying harder to make right choices, surrender your inability to God—become humble, unable—and ask him to begin the process of spiritual growth in you. As you begin to do the hard work of spiritual growth, he will begin reproducing his life in you through the process of internal change. As you cooperate with his pruning and cultivating of your character, you will produce fruit in your season (Ps. 1:3).

Just doing the right thing is more important than why I do it.

It wasn't a happy family that sat in my office. Gerry and Beth Andrews, a couple in their early forties, were on the couch, looking a little bewildered. Across from them sat Dave, their sixteen-year-old son, arms crossed tightly over his chest and head down. He looked like an ad for a Save Our Teens campaign.

During the past few months, Dave had been having trouble at school—skipping classes, displaying a poor attitude when he did attend, making some poor choices of friends. His grades were dropping as a result. School officials had recommended professional help.

I asked Dave what the problem was. A silent stare answered me. I turned to his parents.

"It all started when Dave started spending time with the MacArthur boy down the street," said his father. "He's had lots of . . . you know, problems. Up until that time, our Dave was as bright, responsible, and caring a young man as you'd ever want to meet."

"Dave, what do you think about that?" I asked. Again, the silent stare. So I spoke to the three of them. "Making a poor choice in friends may be part of the problem, but generally things at home contribute to a teen's behavior. How are things between you three?"

Mrs. Andrews spoke up. "Actually, they're fine. We've always been a close Christian family. There's never been much conflict in our home, thank the Lord."

"That's not always a good sign," I said. "People differ about lots of things, and probably need to."

Something woke Dave up out of his staring contest with me. "Ask them about the schedule."

"What schedule?" I asked.

"The one on the refrigerator. That's what's wrong with them. The schedule."

His father leaned forward. "Dave's referring to our weekly family schedule. It's how we keep tabs on our activities. Most families have one."

"So what's the problem with the schedule on the refrigerator?" I asked.

"Everything," Dave said. "Church on Sunday and Wednesdays. I don't like our church. Dinner with the Thompsons on Tuesdays. They're old, and I don't have anything in common with them. Weekends doing projects with Dad."

"What don't you like about all that?"

"They just do things to do things. To keep busy."

"That's not true," piped up Mr. Andrews. "The schedule has always been like that. We've always been active people, and all these activities are good!"

"Yeah?" Dave glared at his father. "I think it's because you and Mom don't like to talk to each other. You keep busy so you don't have to talk to each other."

The room was silent. If you want the unvarnished truth about a family, always ask the black sheep—who has nothing to lose by being honest.

Just Do It

This encounter illustrates a crazymaker that plagues many people: *"Just* doing *the right thing is more important than* why *I do it."* Or, more spiritually phrased: Obedience is the key to the Christian life.

The Andrewses were doing the right things. They were worshiping and fellowshiping and doing things together as a family, but all for the wrong reasons. They were keeping busy only to avoid conflict. The way the Andrewses saw it, God wanted them to obey him for obedience's sake.

Teachers of this crazymaker use passages like this to support their teaching:

> For it is not those who hear the law who are righteous in God's sight, but it is those who obey the law who will be declared righteous. (Rom. 2:13)

> Do not merely listen to the word, and so deceive yourselves. Do what it says. (James 1:22)

God is like the parent who stands over the questioning child and says impatiently, "Just do it!" This view holds that God looks at our *actions* far more than he does our *motives* and internal spiritual state.

Those who hold to the "just-do-it" philosophy are likely to say things like this:

- Go the extra mile whenever anyone asks for help.
- Turn the other cheek any time you are hurt by someone.
- Read the Bible regularly, no matter what.
- Thank God for his provision at all times.
- Obey your authorities in all things without question.
- Stop any gross sins as an act of obedience, including compulsive behaviors (ritualistic, repetitive behaviors) and impulse control problems (addictions to substances, food, sex, spending, etc.).

This concept implies that we do acts of obedience because they're the right things to do, and that God will bless our efforts regardless of our reasons for doing them. If inside you know you're obeying only because you fear being abandoned or looking bad to others, that doesn't matter. It doesn't matter if you're feeling resentment or guilt as you obey. It's your actions that count.

What's So Crazy about This?

As usual, Christians have painted this fallacy with rosy colors. It looks so reasonable. The list above contains many good and important things for Christians to do. Isn't it true that we are to be doers and not just hearers of God's commands? That our behavior does in fact reflect the state of our spiritual lives?

Besides, we all know people who rationalize their sinful behavior:

- "Someone made me do it."
- "I'm a victim of circumstances."
- "With a past like mine, it was inevitable."
- "I couldn't help it."
- "The Devil made me do it."
- "You wouldn't believe how bad traffic was."

Such people are usually shirking their responsibilities and trying to get off the hot seat.

But the Bible won't let them off, for it places a high value on personal responsibility and follow-through. God's followers keep their oaths even when it hurts (Ps. 15:4).

Yet God likes "just do it" obedience as little as he likes lame excuses. Before we look at why, let's see how the Bible defines obedience.

Obedience: Lend Me Your Ear

In both the Old and New Testaments, the words translated "to obey" mean "to hear, to attend to." The Hebrew word *shema* is translated "to hear" more than eight hundred times in the Old Testament; the Greek word *akouō* (as in acoustic guitar) is translated "to hear" some four hundred times in the New Testament. The Bible paints a picture of people paying attention to someone's request or command, then responding.

A couple brought their three-year-old daughter to me because they were concerned about her unresponsiveness. She rarely responded to their directives, often completely ignoring what they said. Something didn't seem right, so I ordered a medical exam for the girl. It turned out that she had a hearing problem. She wasn't disobeying—she simply didn't know she was being addressed.

The biblical idea is this: When we hear, we respond. The Hebrew language doesn't distinguish much between hearing and responding; they go together. For example, the Israelites told Moses, "We will do everything the Lord has said; we will *shema*" (Exod. 24:7). But when they didn't do everything the Lord had said, Isaiah declares: "They would not follow his ways; they did not *shema* his law" (Isa. 42:24). To the Old Testament Jew, if you heard right, you responded right.

The classic Old Testament passage on attentiveness to God is what Jews call "the Great Shema":

> Hear [*shema*], O Israel: The Lord our God, the Lord is one. Love the Lord your God with all your heart and with all your soul and with all your strength. These commandments that I give you today are to be upon your hearts. Impress them on your children. Talk about them when you sit at home and when you walk along the road, when you lie down and when you get up. Tie them as symbols on your hands and bind them on your foreheads. Write them on the doorframes of your houses and on your gates. (Deut. 6:4–8)

Every Jew knew the Shema; the pious still recite it daily. In fact, when asked what the greatest commandment was, Jesus quoted part of this passage—then, echoing Leviticus 19:18, added the second great command: "Love your neighbor as yourself" (Matt. 22:39). All the Law and Prophets can be summarized in these two commandments, Jesus said. If we listen to these principles, we will be the loving people God wants us to be.

Not only do we *shema* God, but he *shemas* us. David cried out to God, "*Shema* me when I call to you, O my righteous God" (Ps. 4:1). "The righteous cry out, and the Lord *shemas* them; he delivers them from all their troubles" (Ps. 34:17). Imagine God bending down to hear our cries for help and then helping us. *Shema* is a two-way street.

We don't see in the Bible the idea of hearing without doing—at least, until Jesus says that "everyone who *akouos* these words of mine and puts them into practice is like a wise man who built his house on the rock" (Matt. 7:24). In the New Testament, hearing God doesn't always guarantee doing what he says.

You remember Rhoda, the servant girl who slammed the door in Peter's face when he showed up unexpectedly after God had miraculously freed him from prison. She's a good example of hearing without doing. She came to *akouo* the door—then, in her excitement, forgot to let Peter into the house (Acts 12:13). She *heard*, but she forgot to *respond* by letting Peter in.

Obedience Always Has a Purpose

Here's the point: The word *obedience* describes a relationship between God and us. We hear what he wants for us, then we respond. Much like a child responds to the voice of his parent, we listen to him and do the right thing.

Why should we obey? Instead of giving the standard circular answer—"Because we should"—the Bible goes deeper than that, to the heart of who we are.

Obedience is a structure to train us in maturity, not an end in itself. Obedience for obedience's sake isn't biblical. Following God's commands always has a purpose.

For example, good parents have one goal in mind for their children: autonomy, or independence. They want their children to learn how to get their needs met, how to be productive, how to solve problems. In the same way, God gives us directives to help us mature and grow up.

Listen to Deuteronomy: "Walk in all the way that the Lord your God has commanded you, *so that you may live and prosper and prolong your days*" (5:33). "The Lord commanded us to obey all these decrees and to fear the Lord our God, *so that we might always prosper and be kept alive*" (6:24). "Observe the Lord's commands and decrees that I am giving you today *for your own good*" (10:13; all italics mine).

God wants us to do the right thing so that we'll grow up. Good parents train kids in talking about their feelings so they can talk to their spouse and friends in adult life. They instruct them in taking out garbage so they can take responsibility for a job when they grow up. They teach them to set appropriate boundaries so they can protect themselves from evil as they grow (Matt. 25:7–9).

You may have been taught that obedience is for obedience's sake—that God wants to be obeyed because he's some sort of control addict. That's not God's fathering style. His directives help us to learn his ways so that we develop into his image. "I will instruct you and teach you in the way you should go," he promises (Ps. 32:8). Obedience is our response to the fathering of God.

Levels of Obedience

Obedience changes as we mature. Our relationships to God and each other require less and less structure as we cultivate more character structure inside. The more we mature, the less specific instruction we need.

A three-year-old, for example, needs to be put to bed. He doesn't realize his biological need for sleep. A fifteen year-old goes to bed (we hope) so she won't miss her ride to school the next day. Spiritual infants need milk; spiritual adults can eat solid food (Heb. 5:12–14). As we grow more mature, we shift from specific commands to a structure for living. We don't need someone to hold our hand through every decision. We're making the Word a part of ourselves: "I have hidden your word in my heart that I might not sin against you" (Ps. 119:11).

Why Obedience for the Sake of Obedience Is Unbiblical

The false assumption "Just doing the right thing is more important than why I do it" has six problems.

This False Assumption Substitutes Sacrifice for True Obedience

If anyone had it together, Jason did—active at church, good job, lovely wife and two children whom he loved, exercised regularly and looked it, kept in close touch with his friends.

But one day, out of the blue, a deep depression hit Jason so heavily he could hardly get out of bed. It made no sense to him. He came to see me.

We talked for a while about Jason's apparently snug and untroubled life before his breakdown. We gradually uncovered that Jason's structured lifestyle was basically a way to fend off a lifelong depression. He had grown up in an alcoholic and abusive family, where he'd lived through all sorts of chaos and crises.

His activity and responsibility saved Jason. Because no one else in the house washed his clothes, prepared meals, and budgeted money, Jason learned to. He became a thirty-year-old at the age of nine.

Jason did the right thing, not because he was selfless and loving, but to stay alive. The depression inevitably caught up with him.

Not that it's unhealthy to be responsible. The *reasons behind the responsibility* are the problem. Jason had lived a lifetime of sacrifice. Fearful of falling apart inside, he stayed busy and active to ward off a breakdown.

Just before coming to me for treatment, in fact, Jason had confided in a Christian friend. "Keep your nose to the grindstone," the friend advised him. "You'll get past it." It didn't work.

Jason stayed busy to avoid dealing with his needs. He wasn't driven to obedience by the love of Christ, but by fear and panic. It was about situations like this that Jesus said, "But go and learn what this means: 'I desire mercy, not sacrifice'" (Matt. 9:13). Our sacrificial, giving, responsible acts are helpful to neither God nor us until we understand God's mercy—being loved just as we are—and then return that love.

A truly responsible lifestyle is the product of being loved just as we are—with our sinfulness, our imperfections, our wounds, and our weaknesses. Then, as we are loved in that state, we learn to give back that love. Jason had not been so loved, and so it was impossible for him to obey in love. He could obey the Bible's commands only because he was told to.

Some people lead highly functional lives not so much to keep their depressions away, but to keep from being shamed by others. I knew a woman who kept her weight in check by being around critical people who would come down on her for gaining weight. When her critical friends moved away one year, this woman put on seventy pounds in several months. The shaming external control hadn't solved the problem—it had just postponed it. She finally lost the weight for the right reasons, but she first had to learn mercy and sacrifice: She had to receive mercy in order to sacrifice her longing for food.

When we do the right thing reluctantly or under compulsion, not freely (2 Cor. 9:6–7), we live in fear. It may be fear of loss, of falling apart, of guilt, or of others' disapproval. But no one can grow or flourish in a fear atmosphere. Love has no place there, for "perfect love drives out fear" (1 John 4:18).

This False Assumption Ignores the Wholeness or Integrity of a Person

Not only do we move away from love when we obey for obedience's sake, but we also become split apart inside. The soul becomes fragmented and disconnected from God. We desire one thing and do another. "These people come near to me with their mouth and honor me with their lips, but their hearts are far from me" (Isa. 29:13).

We were created to be whole, integrated, in body and soul. We are to connect with each other and God this way. When we do, we are loving God with our heart, soul, mind, and strength.

Ever had dinner with someone who didn't want to be there? The conversation may have been pleasant and even interesting, but you sensed that your dinner partner was somewhere else. This splitting brings a lukewarmness to the relationship that prevents true intimacy. That's why God prefers coldness to halfheartedness. An honestly cold heart is in trouble; but because it knows what it is, it can be redeemed. The lukewarm, half-there, half-not-there person, however, is not honest with herself, and so is out of the reach of the grace of God that could heal her.

The "obey for the sake of obedience" idea promotes this sort of split. Rather than exploring why we don't do what we should so that we can work out the conflicts, this crazymaker ignores the problem.

This False Assumption Discourages a Sense of Responsibility

For some time I had been treating Karen, a divorced woman who had just started to re-enter the Christian dating world (a dangerous place, as those in it are aware). She had begun dating Bernie, despite the fact that he frequently stood her up—but always with a good explanation.

Karen asked me if I would see them together for a few sessions. First, though, I wanted to meet Bernie alone for a diagnostic evaluation.

At first glance, Bernie was the nicest guy you could imagine. Good-looking and in his midthirties, he was as attentive and helpful a client as a therapist could ask for. Too much so, it turned out. Bernie was a "nodder," so eager to please that he agreed with my statements before I finished them. When I mentioned this to him, he eagerly agreed that he had that trait!

"Can you help me with it, Doc?" he asked. "I'll do anything you say to work on it."

Bernie had a history of failed relationships and unsuccessful career moves. He jumped in with 150 percent enthusiasm, energy, and eagerness to please—until conflicts came, that is, when Bernie would bail out. That's what eventually happened with Karen. One day he pulled a permanent no-show, and she never heard from him again.

Bernie wanted to do it right—at least on the outside. I have no doubt that he was sincere about his desires. However, he was so concerned with pleasing me and others that he wouldn't take responsibility for his true feelings about situations.

That's the second problem with the "just do it" crazymaker: It discourages responsibility for one's own actions and attitudes. The person becomes so focused on pleasing the feared authority—God, parent, boss, spouse—he isn't able to deal with differences.

One of the marks of maturity is moving from unconscious to conscious choices. We move out of the automatic, learned habits of relating and responding to biblically driven decisions. Bernie was still bound to the frightened and anxious way of relating he had learned as a child. He couldn't slow down from external pleasing to determine what he really thought and felt about situations. His actions (not showing up at appointed times and disappearing from time to time) shed light on his true values.

Don't ask why. People under the burden of the "just do it" crazymaker aren't free to ask why. Asking questions is considered rebellious, defiant, and insubordinate. Obedience, they feel, should be automatic and unquestioned.

Yet to forbid questions greatly discourages the formation of responsibility in believers. Adults want to know why, not to get around obedience, but to learn and grow. They like having the big picture. And while God alone has the big picture, in the Scriptures he allows his children to ask why. Asking why allows us to work together with God (Phil. 2:12–13).

Successful executives are aware that their top producers are people who frequently ask why. They aren't content to perform their tasks by rote. They want the wisdom of the boss's perspective to help them achieve their goals. They know that this is best for the boss, the company, and themselves.

The word *why* occurs more than four hundred times in the Bible. God himself asks us "Why?" to make us think. "Why are you angry?" God asked Cain. "Why is your face downcast?" (Gen. 4:6). God wanted Cain to gain insight into his unhappiness—a value hardly encouraged by the "just do it" idea.

Jesus also responded to many whys posed to him: "How is it that we and the Pharisees fast, but your disciples do not fast?" (Matt. 9:14). "Why couldn't we drive [the demon] out?" (Matt. 17:19). "Why this waste?" (referring to the woman who poured expensive perfume on Jesus' head in Matthew 26:8). He answered these and many more questions, knowing that information helps adults to take more responsibility.

Beware of authority figures who demand instant, unquestioned obedience. Not only do they *not* represent the character of God, but they probably also have something to lose (such as control over you) by your having information.

This False Assumption Promotes Lying

Remember the story of the little boy who didn't obey his father's directive to sit down? No matter what his dad did to persuade him, he refused to comply. In frustration, his father finally picked up his son and placed him, bottom down, on the sofa.

"Now you're sitting," said Dad.

"I'm sitting on the outside," replied his unbroken son, "but I'm standing on the inside!"

That anecdotal boy was honest about his rebellion. Advocates of "just do it," on the other hand, must lie about their true feelings. In other words, we often feel resentment, resistance, or rebellion about doing the right thing. It's part of our heritage, part of being Adam and Eve's children. When we must comply on the outside, however, our rebellion moves from light and openness to hiding, where it is much more difficult to resolve.

In the parable about a dad and his two sons, the second son was a liar. When his father told him, "Son, go and work today in the vineyard," he answered, " 'I will, sir,' but he did not go" (Matt. 21:28, 30). Jesus then told the crowd that the tax collectors and prostitutes were entering the kingdom of God ahead of those who were like that son.

Why did Jesus give priority to two such unlovable groups as these? Because they couldn't hide their weaknesses and needs. Tax collectors and prostitutes were constantly in public shame because of their vocations. And that was Jesus' point: Whatever is out in the open, exposed to the light of relationship, can be healed. Whatever is hidden—even under a show of compliance—will stay unhealed because it is disowned.

What do you do when you're asked to do the right thing? Do you make a deliberate, thought-out, free choice to say yes or no? Or do you lie about the no inside you, and say yes? Unless you can say no, you cannot truly say yes to God or people.

This False Assumption Denies Our Fallenness

At its heart, "just do it" means, "You can obey" or "The reason you don't obey is that you don't want to."

Over and over again we hear Christian teachers, preachers, and counselors make the mistaken assumption that once we are believers, we can do anything.

"To believe that people can't obey every command of Scripture at any given moment," a church elder told me, "is to impugn the character of God." He believed that obedience is simply a matter of submission and will.

The biblical truth, however, is the opposite. The Bible is full of hope for those who realize that we can't live perfect lives. We lie to ourselves when "we claim to be without sin" (1 John 1:8). We struggle with the truth that "what I want to do I do not do, but what I hate I do" (Rom. 7:15). And yet Jesus blessed our poverty of spirit (Matt. 5:3)

God has a great deal of room in his heart for those who fail and sin, over and over. He cares for those of us who admit we can't "just do it."

This False Assumption Devalues the Power of the Cross in Our Lives

In my first-grade year, our family moved with my dad's business. As happens with lots of six-year-olds who suffer the trauma of moving and switching schools, I [John] had trouble with my reading.

Needless to say, my parents were concerned. My mom hovered over me anxiously as I read my assignments at home after school. It wasn't helpful to either of us. With her standing over my shoulder, I was doubly anxious as I read. If I missed a word, she corrected it instantly. We danced this high-anxiety duet for weeks, until one day when my mom consulted *her* mother, who had raised six children. Granny had some advice for her.

After school the next day, I arrived home to the usual milk and cookies on the kitchen table. And my mother, as usual, asked me to read to her. Reluctantly, I pulled out my primer and began.

But something was different this time. Instead of sitting behind me, reading along, Mom stayed at the sink, washing dishes with her back to me. I'd read for a while, starting and halting, wrestling with the words.

Mom didn't say a word until I asked her for help, then she'd offer an answer. And on I'd go.

It worked. I relaxed after a while and stopped worrying about the mistakes. I even enjoyed the little reading I was doing. What was helping was that Mom seemed more at ease, more casual, standing over there at the sink.

I didn't know until years later that the whole time I was reading, she was standing there silently, tears running down her cheeks. Her empathy for my struggle was great, and her motherly instincts pressed her to rescue me. Yet she stayed quiet and kept her voice calm, so I wouldn't know. I've been a voracious reader ever since.

"Just do it" didn't work for me. It was a demand I couldn't satisfy. I had no safe place to struggle or work on my deficits. What worked was Mom giving me grace to make mistakes, with no anxiety, condemnation, or guilt—but lots of cookies and milk.

The Safety Net Called Grace

Perhaps the most serious problem of the "just do it" idea is that it leaves little room for the gift of life bought by Christ's death. Maturity is a cycle of trying and failing our way into growth. The cycle goes like this:

1. You try.
2. You fail.
3. You receive grace and forgiveness.
4. You suffer consequences.
5. You learn from the consequences.
6. You try.
7. You do a little better.
8. You fail.

And so on. We learn by practice, says Hebrews 5:14. When we know that we won't be condemned when we fail, we grow faster. We take more risks. But living under the "just do it" bondage dooms us to not learn from our mistakes. The "just do it" fallacy at its best interrupts and at its worst destroys the maturity cycle. Grace, on the other hand, protects us from loss of love as we mature through trying and failing.

When is the last time you backed away from a struggle with compulsive behaviors? Were you bound and determined to beat it through discipline, guilt, or self-shaming?

There's a better way. When we allow ourselves to work through our inner motives and conflicts about situations, we are more free to be autonomous, to take responsibility for our behavior, and to be truly free in Christ.

If I know the truth, I will grow.

She was at the end of her therapy. The journey had been difficult. When Joyce began therapy, she was a hundred and thirty pounds overweight. Now, after lots of hard work, she had returned to a normal weight.

Her weight problem was, of course, only a symptom of deeper problems. In therapy, she had had to face some painful truths and realities about her life, and do some difficult work in her relationships.

The hard work had started when she realized how much her parents had controlled her as a child. She idealized them, constantly caved in to their wishes, was unable to stand up to them and be her own boss. In short, she had little control over her choices and opinions.

This pattern of control had spilled over into her adult relationships. Her sisters and friends generally ran her life, and she smiled every step of the way—the consummate servant, gladly doing whatever anyone wanted her to do. But she gradually began resenting deeply the very people she apparently loved and served so gladly.

In addition to recognizing her relationship problems, Joyce finally remembered her sexual abuse when she was eight. The depression and grief she experienced as an adult at first overwhelmed her. She endured a period of anxiety and even panic because she was afraid people could see the shameful truth.

But Joyce hung in there, faithfully working on whatever it seemed God was trying to show her next. She established better boundaries with her parents: She gave them a firm no when they wanted something from her she didn't want to give, and she dealt with the conflict that followed such refusals. (This was the most difficult part of her therapy.) Her parents wondered what had happened to their dependable daughter. Why the sudden selfishness? They poured on the guilt, but Joyce stood firm.

She began opening up to people about the pain of her childhood sexual abuse, allowing others to be there for her and to comfort her. She slowly learned to depend on people in a way that she never imagined she could. As she developed a support system, the inner emptiness that had compelled her to eat (one of the symptoms of her woundedness) began to be replaced with love.

When she started to see me, Joyce had subscribed to all twelve false assumptions. Yet her healing had come in a different way than her assumptions had predicted. One day towards the end of her treatment, I asked Joyce how she explained her weight loss, a very visible symbol of her increasing healthiness.

"I used to think that if I knew the Bible, studied it, and depended on it to transform me, my problems would be solved," she replied. "But it didn't work.

"Here's what did work: First, I had to come out of isolation and learn to connect with other people. In the beginning I did that with you, and then I was able to do it with others.

"Second, I had to set boundaries in order to control my life. As long as others had control over me—and I didn't—I didn't have the self-control I needed to say no to food.

"Third, I had to learn to deal with and express my pain and hurt, instead of covering it up with eating. When I learned that pain could be my friend instead of my enemy, I was not so afraid to face it, and it began to go away. Now when I'm hurt, instead of eating a large pizza, I call someone and talk it out.

"What I've really learned in all this, though, is that what I thought about the Bible is not true. Bible study didn't cure me. I learned that I have to *do* what the Bible talks about. Studying the Bible told me what I needed to do, but only in actually getting out there and *doing* those things did I see what the Bible was actually talking about. Knowing the Bible did not change me, doing it did."

I was struck by how her view of the Bible had changed. Joyce didn't believe the Bible any less. To the contrary, she believed it more, because she had proved its power in her life. She had been taught that Bible study, that "knowing the truth," would change her. Yet she discovered that doing the truth was what made her grow.

When we were young counselors, a strong movement was just beginning in the evangelical church to apply biblical truth to emotional problems. People were being taught that Scripture memory, exegetical teaching, doctrinal purity, and personal Bible study were the keys to spiritual and emotional growth.

This focus is still popular. If they simply know their Bibles, many Christians are taught, their emotional problems will be cured. They are taught that knowing God's Word is the all-sufficient cure for everything that ails them. Bible study and prayer, this camp believes, are the answers to emotional problems.

Proponents of this view point to Jesus' words: "The truth will set you free" (John 8:32), as well as some of the descriptive passages about the Scriptures, such as

Psalm 19:7–14, or Psalm 119. From such passages they build an entire system that relies upon Bible study and truth as the cure for everything.

This approach sounds good. What could sound more Christian than to stand up for the integrity of the Word of God? How could anyone even question such teaching? It sounds like heresy to even ask, "Is the Bible enough?"

We believe that the Bible is God's Word and that its revelation is sufficient. What we question is its application. Is the cure simply reading the Bible and learning truth? The false assumption here is, "If I know God's truth, I will grow." Yet we believe that Bible study alone was never God's remedy for emotional and spiritual problems. Healing takes work.

This false assumption has been popular for centuries. One of Job's friends offered him the same advice: "Submit to God and be at peace with him; in this way prosperity will come to you. Accept instruction from his mouth and lay up his words in your heart" (Job 22:21–22). Job's suffering would end, his friend assured him, if only Job understood the truth and aligned himself with it. Yet God rebuked the friend for giving Job such erroneous advice.

"You diligently study the Scriptures," Jesus said to those well-acquainted with the Scriptures, "because you think that by them you possess eternal life. These are the Scriptures that testify about me" (John 5:39). The Jewish leaders were so busy studying the minutia of Scripture that they didn't recognize the One to whom the Scriptures were pointing, the One who could lead them into the spiritual life that truly heals.

We are not saying that the Word is dispensable for spiritual growth. It is not. But neither is Bible study the entire picture. The Scriptures themselves teach that Bible study is necessary yet insufficient in itself for leading one into a healthy Christian life.

The Absence of Relationship

Truth alone saves no one. The Pharisees had all the truth they needed. What they didn't have were relationships with God and with each other.

The essential problem is that we are alienated from God and others. The essence of the spiritual life is to be reconciled to God and have a vibrant relationship with him (2 Cor. 5:18–19), and then to be reconciled to friends and neighbors in the same way: To love God with all your being and to love others as yourself.

God with Skin On

"Don't be afraid of the dark, honey," said a mother, calming her frightened child. "God is with you." To which the child replied, "But I need somebody with skin on."

We talk continually about how relationship with God is essential for emotional growth—but so do those who teach the false assumptions. Yet though they teach that prayer and Bible study are healing agents, their emphasis on Bible study (and relationship to God through Bible study) falls short of what the Bible actually teaches—an *incarnational* gospel. This means that for us to realize the grace of God, God had to put skin on. He had to become a man. Even now, he comes to be with us in bodily form through his church, which we call the *body* of Christ. The church is Christ with skin on. We feel the grace of God not only by studying about it in the Bible, but by experiencing it incarnationally, just as it was first revealed.

In our hospital program, Phyllis was a patient who had been an active Christian worker her entire adult life. Yet at age forty-five, she had gotten so depressed she could no longer function.

When we put her into a group, a pattern emerged:

Every time a group member started talking about a problem in order to get feedback and support from the group, Phyllis quoted a Bible verse to him. No one told his or her story without a Scripture quote from Phyllis.

Patients and staff quickly realized two things—Phyllis had an amazing grasp of the Bible, and she had virtually no ability to relate intimately with others.

Consequently, Phyllis was very alone inside. She knew a lot about God's love, but experienced very little. Extremely cut off from other people emotionally, she became depressed. Phyllis was trying to have a relationship with God apart from his body (the church), and it wasn't working.

The apostle John wrote about a relationship with God apart from his church: "For anyone who does not love his brother, whom he has seen, cannot love God, whom he has not seen" (1 John 4:20). We need God "with skin on," and that is the function of the body of Christ. "Above all, love each other deeply, because love covers over a multitude of sins. Offer hospitality to one another without grumbling. Each one should use whatever gift he has received to serve others, faithfully administering God's grace in its various forms" (1 Peter 4:8–10). Humans are God's agents for administering his grace.

God's grace is not something that we learn only by reading the Bible. We also realize it in human relationships.

Healing Hands of Humans, Too

Truth without relationship sidesteps the healing God wants for us in his body. Christians are told to study the Bible for their growth and comfort, but the Bible they read instructs them to return to human relationships for healing: Go and abide with one another, comfort one another, weep with those who weep, confront one another, confess to one another, encourage one another, and build one another up. These relational elements are essential for growth and transformation in the soul.

> We will in all things grow up into him who is the Head, that is, Christ. From him the whole body, joined and held together by every supporting ligament, *grows and builds itself up in love,* as each part does its work. (Eph. 4:15–16, italics mine)

The teaching "If I just know the truth, I will grow" clearly contradicts the biblical mandate to go to the body of Christ for growth. You can't read the Bible and think that it says that studying it is enough. It points to Jesus and a relationship with him and his people.

Doing the Truth

Another reason this false assumption is harmful is that it teaches against the very truth it says to study. God designed sanctification, which has several elements beyond Bible study and learning the truth. These elements involve practicing the truth: putting the Bible down and going and doing what it says to do:

> Do not merely listen to the word, and so deceive yourselves. Do what it says. Anyone who listens to the word but does not do what it says is like a man who looks at his face in a mirror and after looking at himself, goes away and immediately forgets what he looks like. But the man who looks intently into the perfect law that gives freedom and continues to do this, not forgetting what he has heard, but doing it—he will be blessed in what he does. (James 1:22–25)

In other words, James says, "Put your Bible down and go do it!" Jesus told his listeners the same thing:

Why do you call me "Lord," and do not do what I say?
I will show you what he is like who comes to me and
hears my words and puts them into practice. He is
like a man building a house who dug down deep and
laid the foundation on rock. When a flood came, the
torrent struck that house but could not shake it,
because it was well built. But the one who hears my
words and does not put them into practice is like a
man who built a house on the ground without a
foundation. The moment the torrent struck that
house, it collapsed and its destruction was complete.
(Luke 6:46–49)

These passages compare hearers of the Word with
those who practice it. Christ dismisses the value of
merely hearing his Word.

People who are taught to get over their emotional
problems by just reading their Bibles and praying are
being taught to become *hearers* of the Word. There will
be no genuine healing, however, until they become
doers of the Word. Bible study alone has been lifted to a
status the Bible never intended. God says the Bible is
important because it points us to Jesus and tells us how
to live out our relationship with God and others—in
fact, it serves as a guide for living our whole life.

Though she had been in various types of Christian
service for years, Terri became, inexplicably, suicidally
depressed during a two-month missionary assignment.
She soon learned the first steps of expressing her pain
in therapy and letting others comfort her. She learned
to be honest with God and cultivate a relationship with
him. She worked on forgiving people against whom she
had held deep grudges. She got reconnected to the
body of Christ.

As Terri's depression lifted and her relationship
with God improved, she began to grow in her love for
God instead of feeling duty-bound to serve him.

Then something happened. Terri appeared in my office one day, very scared, distant, and confused.

"I don't know if I can trust you anymore," she said tearfully. "I just met with my former spiritual teacher, and she said you were heretical."

"What did she mean by that?" I asked her.

"She said that you were a secular humanist and that I shouldn't see you anymore or listen to what you say."

"What did she say that you should do instead?" I was concerned because I knew that, although she had made great gains, Terri wasn't finished with therapy.

"She said that I needed to get back to the Bible and depend on it only, that the Bible was sufficient for all my troubles. She said that counseling was godless, and that if I read the Bible and memorized the truth, it would set me free."

"I want you to think hard, Terri. How would you describe what you have been doing in therapy?"

"What do you mean?"

"What have you learned and done since you have been seeing me?"

"To get in touch with my grief. That I need to forgive. I've opened up to other people and let them support me. I've tried to separate from my mother so I could have a better relationship with my husband. Tried to be more honest about what I struggle with by confiding in others. Tried to be more honest with God."

"Now let's look more closely at the work you have been doing and compare it with what the Bible teaches," I said. "Solomon and Paul talk about grief. Jesus and Paul talk about forgiveness. Jesus, Paul, Peter, David, and John urge their listeners to connect with other people for support. Genesis speaks of leaving and cleaving, and Jesus says that you may end up being enemies with your own family members when you begin to do what he says.

"Both Paul and James," I continued, "write about

being honest and confessing to others our shortcomings, feelings, and sins. And Job and Jesus stressed
honest relationships with God. It sounds to me that you
have been doing exactly what the Bible tells you to do,
and that is why you are getting better.

"Therapy has been the place where you have been
doing what God commands. Sounds to me like your
former spiritual teacher wants you to just read the Bible
without doing what it says."

"I guess I really am doing what it says," Terri said
slowly. "But she seems so spiritual ... and I get
confused ..."

"I have no intention of trying to control you, Terri. I
want you to see some other people and tell them
everything that we do here, then get their input. Then
go home and read your Bible as I've suggested in the
past. Finally, think about whether you want to continue
with your therapy—or to follow her advice and teachings. I want it to be your decision. And I want you to
make sure you talk to a couple of pastors in the process,
telling them exactly what you've been doing."

Terri soon got back on track, practicing those actions
that had been helping her—but not without much fear
of disobeying her spiritual mentor.

Real problems arise when people in counseling are
doing the hard work of therapy and then one of their
spiritual teachers condemns what they are working on,
calling it "secular humanism." They are then instructed
to get back to "biblical" ways of healing—Bible study
and prayer.

When they study their Bible, they find that it says to
do the things they were doing in therapy—take responsibility for what is inside, uncover the darkness, grieve,
forgive, reconcile, learn, confront, express feelings,
confess, and support.

This is exactly what is so ridiculous about the false
assumption "If I know the truth, I will grow." It tells

people to study their Bible, yet prevents them from doing what it says.

Character Change

Character change—to be transformed into God's likeness—is the key to real healing for all of us (2 Cor. 3:18).

But such transformation is hard work. It comes not by simply memorizing Scripture and trying to be inundated with truth. That is the Pharisees' method. Real character change comes from practicing the truth, not just hearing it. People who are actively involved in recovery and character change are doing the hard work of denying themselves. They should not be told to stop doing the truth, and instead just to study it or listen to it in exegetical sermons.

Actually doing leads one to become humble and loving, responsible and forgiving, cleansed and transformed—and actively involved in bringing others into the same kind of healing (2 Cor. 1:3–4). Learn the truth, study your Bible diligently, but don't stop there. Take what it says and put it into action by practicing the healing process it points to. Holding to his teaching, not just knowing it, sets you free (John 8:31–32).

Jesus always emphasized doing what he said: "But the seed on good soil stands for those with a noble and good heart, who hear the word, retain it, and by persevering produce a crop" (Luke 8:15). If we sincerely do this, we become like him who said, "I do know him and keep his word" (John 8:55). And in keeping his word, there is life and health indeed.

"How can a young man keep his way pure? By living according to your word. . . . I rejoice in following your statutes as one rejoices in great riches" (Ps. 119:9, 14).

Conclusion

We have one regret in writing this book. It's incomplete.

These twelve false assumptions are the major growth teachings with which the church struggles, but more are created all the time. As a seminary professor remarked, "Our ability to sin creatively is limited only by our depravity."[1]

What's a Christian to do?

1. *Seek God and ask him to illuminate your thinking with his truth and wisdom.* If the teaching is accurate, God wants you to understand that he is the fount from which all truth flows.

2. *Make the Bible your final authority.* Don't let religious-sounding jargon, high I.Q., eloquence, authority, or sincerity determine if a teaching is true. Test the spirits with the Word of God. And when you read the Bible, look up the verses in several translations. Check out the context. Does the idea fit in the passage? Learn to be an independent student of the Bible. There are many good commentaries, dictionaries, and Bible study aids in Christian bookstores. And enroll in a Bible study methods class offered by a church (yours or another).

3. *Learn to think critically.* In other words, don't believe something just because an authority figure says it (including us). Beware of teachers who are threatened by your questions. Jesus answered people's questions; the Pharisees were insulted by them.

4. *Spend time with people who think for themselves.* Learn what questions they ask when they read new

information. Mavericks often find nuggets of gold that party-line people miss out on because they're stuck in tradition.

5. *Ask yourself if you believe something because you were taught it, or because it's true.* Many people don't question false assumptions because they might shake up their loyalty to their family, church, or community. Remember that God's truth will always win out.

6. *Look at the fruit of the teaching.* Does it lead to love, responsibility, self-control, and forgiveness? Or does it bring on isolation, compulsion, guilt, and shame?

Our prayer is that you will dig underneath every false assumption to the truth—and, in the truth, find Jesus.

Henry Cloud, Ph.D.
John Townsend, Ph.D.
Minirth-Meier Clinic West
260 Newport Center Drive #430
Newport Beach, CA 92660
1-800-877-HOPE

Endnotes

Assumption #3
1. See also *Changes That Heal* (Grands Rapids: Zondervan, 1990, 1992), by Henry Cloud, and *Hiding from Love* (Colorado Springs: NavPress, 1991) pp. 59–118, by John Townsend, for a complete discussion of these developmental stages.
2. For more information on boundaries, see *Boundaries: When to Say Yes, When to Say No to Take Control of Your Life* by Henry Cloud and John Townsend (Grand Rapids: Zondervan, 1992).

Assumption #4
1. See *Hiding from Love*, pp. 49–54.

Assumption #6
1. You will get a feel for how pervasive God's warning against generational sin is if you look up the word *fathers* in an exhaustive concordance.

Assumption #7
1. See the sections on bonding in *Changes That Heal* and *Hiding from Love* for more on this subject.
2. Laird Harris, Gleason L. Archer, Jr. and Bruce K. Waltke, *Theological Wordbook of the Old Testament* (Chicago: Moody Press, 1980), 1:570.

Assumption #9
1. Conversation with Jack Deere, Dallas Theological Seminary, 1979.

Conclusion
1. John Hannah, class on church history, Dallas Theological Seminary, 1978.